NESTING IN NATURE

SANJAY PATIL

I have no special talents.
I am only passionately curious...

Sanjay Patil

Published by:

BNCA
PUBLICATION CELL

C/o Maharshi Karve Stree Shikshan Samstha's
Dr. Bhanuben Nanavati College of Architecture
for Women
Karvenagar, Pune 411052
T: 91-20-25474060 / 25476966
email: mail@bnca.ac.in

SUPER BOOK HOUSE

Super Book House
3A/4, Sind Chambers, Colaba Causeway,
Mumbai, Maharashtra 400005
Tel: 022-22020106/22830446
Cell: 09930009369
Email:superbookhouse@gmx.com

email: arsanjaypatil@gmail.com
web: www.environplanners.com

ISBN: 978-93-81452-02-8

Conceptualizer and Creative Editor:
Ritu Sharma
Author:
Minaz Ansari
Design and Layout:
Designatwork Technologies Pvt Ltd, Pune
Prashant Jadhav , Bluesky Communications
Midas Touch, Nashik
Photographs & Images:
Hemant Patil, Atul Kanetkar, Sanjay Patil
Illustrations:
Uday Ahire

Price: Rs. 3500

CONTENT

PREFACE
Sanjay Patil 8

BEYOND THE RIM
Christopher C. Benninger 10

HUMAN CENTRIC SPACES
Anand Mahindra 14

THE VALUES TO ADORE
Anurag Kashyap 18

IN HIS WORDS
Minaz Ansari 22

COURTYARDS WHICH LIVE 30
Minaz Ansari

NASHIK MAP INDICATING THE LOCATIONS OF VARIOUS PROJECTS COVERED IN THE BOOK

PROJECTS :

Masani Residence 38
Mahindra Management Development Centre 48
Architect's Own Workspace 60
Mahindra Institute of Quality 70
Kusumagraj Memorial 86
Farmhouse at Mahiravani 98
Bapat Bagwe Farmhouse 114
Rasne Residence 126
Raosaheb Patil Residence 136
Bhujbal Knowledge City 146
Goliya Residence 162
Suryawanshi Residence 172
Sandip Foundation 184
Workspace For Mr. Bhujbal 200
Beyond Resort 212
Y.C.M.O.U. Library 228
Adaptive Reuse - Papaya Nursery 240
Workspace for Green Space Realtors 250
Bagad Residence 262

AWARDS AND ACHIEVEMENTS 276

PUBLISHED WORKS 277

Sanjay Patil

PREFACE

Knowledge sharing is integral to me and has always given me great pleasure and satisfaction. A large part of my study in life has come out of my quest for learning from the environment, places and the people around me; whether it has to do with architecture or other allied arts. And therefore I have always made a conscious effort to share with others the little bit that I have learnt through my work, travel and other hobbies.

This book is just an extension of this love for sharing; a humble effort to document some of my works across the last three decades and present it to a wider audience. I also hope that this book motivates many other accomplished names in the architectural circle to come out and publish their works.

I have no special talents. I am only passionately curious.

This book is an honest endeavor to make the reader a part of the design process and my passion for my work that is so much a part of my being. I hope to share my belief in sustainable design, respect for the past and love for nature through a cross section of projects ranging from individual residences to institutes and other public spaces.

In this journey my appreciation goes to all my clients who have trusted me and endowed confidence in me to build a conducive environment for their purpose; to all the consultants whose contribution was crucial in various aspects of the projects; to the contractors, supervision engineers and artisans who did remarkable work in all the projects within the scheduled time; to all the people in my office and outside the office who worked for the projects.

To Minaz Ansari, who triggered this idea of a book long back and supported by her poetic write ups; Ritu Sharma, who mobilised this idea and took up this task towards realisation with her perseverance and with support of Dr. Anurag Kashyap, Principal 'Bhanuben Nanavati College of Architecture for Women' in Pune and its publication cell; To all my photographer friends for documenting all the projects; Jaidev Ranade who is instrumental in designing this book and inducing confidence in us; to Prof. Yashwant Pitkar who introduced me to Mr. Husain Lehri of Super Book House who agreed for the joint publication and distribution of the book.

I am grateful to Padmashree Ar. B.V. Doshi Sir for being a critic and guide throughout this journey. I am thankful to Ar. Christopher Benninger for his constructive inputs towards this publication and Mr. Anand Mahindra for sharing his insight.

Last but not least, my supporting family and friends.

I am also happy that the projects in this book present glimpses of Nashik - my birthplace, my home and a city I have always loved. For it is in this native soil, that my dreams found roots and my passion spread its wings. In gratitude to all those who have been a part of it, I present my journey so far.

Thank you.

Page 4,5: Light and shadow create patterns in the entrance lobby at the Beyond Resort.
Left: A placid lily pond at the architect's farmhouse.

Christopher Charles Benninger

BEYOND THE RIM

Sanjay Patil was born in the small town of Nashik lying comfortably away from the influences of the great metropolises of India. He and his town grew up together into a man and a city. Maturing in a relatively remote environment, Sanjay evolved his own personality and concepts in a setting where few people had ever heard of architecture, much less fretted over the fads and fancies of bourgeoning consumerism. Lying just four hours by train up the mountains from Mumbai, the mercantile center of India, where new styles imported from Paris, London and Manhattan tell people what to wear, which label to check and 'what's in,' Nashik awoke gradually to globalization.

This gradual, yet steady, awakening fed the young architect with a variety of commissions without clouding his mind with preconceived follies. Nashik's location gifted its population a kind of benign neglect and innocence, liberating it from the straight jackets of disruptive, alien glitter and the inane styles influencing India's Eurocentric metropolises. Deconstructivist, Post Modernist and Critical Regionalist theories and labels, born from frenetic intellectual competition and the ideological inebriation of the West, were only the dribble of pseudo-intellectuals in India. Alien theories, Mickey Mouse caps, New Age beliefs and Old Spice underarm deodorants, all arrived through media-driven peer group pressures and hot air ad-men, luring youth and tempering the imaginations of Generation X, who wanted to 'get it right,' and be 'with it!'

Sanjay's imagination was left free to grow on its own; to define itself, to be fluid and to drift in serendipity innocence; maybe never to get homogenized, amalgamated and gelled into the global mould!

In America, the Walt Disney Company perfected something I call 'imagineering.' They can design and engineer people's imaginations! Disney designed, packaged and marketed artificial realities that had never existed, fabricating make-believe realities through animated films. In the 1990's Disney took their fabricated dreams off the silver screen and brought them into the streets of America. In Disney's gated communities, people could live the Disney World illusions and fantasies, in place of their own personalities!

The Walt Disney Company and hundreds of

others in Hollywood, in Manhattan, in Milan, Paris, London and Tokyo produced and labeled 'imaginations' for people to buy in place of their own life-journeys of self-discovery.

Megalopolis invented hyper-reality products, exchanging boring reality for make-believe experiences. Celebration, the New Urbanist real-estate development in Florida, offers clients an option of cashing in their own imaginations for the virtual reality of a once-upon-a-time imaginary 'Small American Town.' The camaraderie of casually chatting with friends on streets and in cafes is replaced with animal friends. Donald Duck and Mickey Mouse, in which life becomes a fable of truths spoken by anthropomorphic cartoons, are placed as fiberglass manikins about the town, some doubling up as trash bins!

In this construct of 'virtually imagineered minds,' filled with a hunger for consuming branded dreams, buying Chinese made bric-a-brac, carrying Louis Vuitton and Gucci bags, defacing oneself with Revlon lipstick, and disguising one's natural aroma with Gillette sprays, an architecture of nothingness has emerged. Glass boxes, gingerbread front porches, cute little things, decorated facades, all environmentally certified, looking like wood, but made of PVC! Fakery and the artificial permeate the ambiance.

In this construct, where the cultural epicenters are frantically reaching out their octopus-like arms into ever expanding cultural realms, marketing their vapid nothingness through rings and layers, out to peripheries through managers and ads, the world's imagination is being transformed! In this world of branding, labeling, media and marketing, a new construct of the twentieth-first century imagination has matured. Old myths, fables and folklore have been replaced with contrived and designed imaginary products, responding to imaginary needs. You can now buy your personality, mail-order your inner sense of self, choose a spiritual system on the web, window-shop for smiles and grins! You can SEEM to be whatever you want to BE. You can choose your personae from supermarket displays, and compose your own little you, but all made from pre-imagined, off-the-shelf images and dreams.

Imploding forces gather at the global cultural epicenters, under humongous marketing gravitational forces, leaving free energy floating randomly out on the far-off edges. In this construct one can see the world of dreaming of millions and billions of human imaginations, within a structure of circles, each drawn out around the others in concentric rings, all influenced by ideas emanating out from the center.

As one moves from the outer circles back inward towards the center, the 'imagineering of the mind' becomes more intense and constraining! One's imagination becomes a prison from which there is no escape. In this construct, the center is an intense, all-enveloping molten drug, generated by workaholic zombies, driven by man-eat-man competition, ruthless greed and rampant desires; all driving fabricated ideas and newly contrived concepts; all competing to be the next 'big seller!'

As one nears the center of this cultural meltdown there is a high density of ambitious young designers, elbowing one another, running toward the center, clambering over each other and clawing their way to dominance, only for the few winners to be branded and broadcast back out, back into the vast consumer markets of the mind. Every season needs a 'new concept' leaving aside piles of failures, last year's worn-out fads, all lying in heaps beside the alter of fame and wealth!

Fashion houses and 'style studios' architects, elite galleries, design journals, architectural critics, documentary films, and 'the design business' are all branding what's right and rubbishing what's out of style - wrong!

The center is obstreperously dictating and directing its commands of what is good and what is bad, out to the furthest reaches, ring by ring, across cultures and economic systems.

Finally, like the waves of a stone thrown into a still pond, the ripples, somewhere beyond the last rim of the fashionable, disappear into the vast universe of the real. In that objective reality beyond the edge, Sanjay Patil grew his own imagination, design concepts and his architecture!

In this center-periphery construct, a nucleus of hyperinteractive global mega-metropolises lie at the molten core, the burning hot nucleus of competition, screaming and yelling through advertisements, film, music, fiction, news, fashion, art, poetry and politically correct thinking to dominate the world's boundaries of questioning, thinking and even of 'imagining'! Around this center, secondary clusters catalyzing secondary circles feed a sphere of mirrored fashions.

Yet a step further out, another imaginary loci of the old port cities of Miami, Caracas, Rio and Buenos Aires, Cape Town, Durban, Mombasa, Istanbul, Cairo, Mumbai, Colombo, Chennai, Kolkata, Rangoon, Singapore, Jakarta, Sydney, Hong Kong, Shanghai and Osaka form a third imaginary concentric circle of influence, sucking its ideas out from the center and vomiting their own magic spells on thinking within their own hinterlands of thought and creativity.

Provincial cultural centers, within the forth ring, like Pune, Bengaluru, Hyderabad, Lucknow and Ahmedabad in India, lie still further out towards a frayed imaginary edge, yet vibrating with half-baked western theories, principles, axioms and ideas, with less fanaticism and intensity. Yet they still spit out the clichés, ideas and concepts they're told are true and beautiful, returning home at night to their Apple Macs, Heineken beer and plagiarized television serials, wearing faded jeans and baseball caps turned backwards.

Then further out into the vast archipelago of smaller towns, where an occasional fake Gucci or counterfeit Levis will do, in a fifth ring, still another faint circle catches only small beeps of the hallucinating correct way to 'be,' and finally the energy dissipates off into the rustic villages, and into the wildernesses of mankind's imaginations, where an ancient rhythm, with its own primordial beat, fills the air with a beautiful emptiness. This emptiness is called civilization!

As one moves out, further and further, over one edge and across to another, jumping from rim to rim, the entrapping knowledge and the magnetic pull of the dominating center dissipates and finally disappears, waning into a wonderful blissfulness. In this emptiness and peace the mind is free, and imaginations wander here and there in the forests of creative nothingness. There are no templates, icons, masters, journals, critics or great universities telling little minds what they should think as they mature, and telling people 'who they should be.'

It is here, out on 'the edge' of the mumbo jumbo world of fashion that Sanjay Patil evolved, in relative freedom from the disruptions of fads, styles and fancies; free to swim in the fluid context of his projects and the real needs of his patrons.

I see in this document, in this archive of Sanjay Patil's life work, the 'sketches' of his own imaginary journey to self-discovery. His design process was born from small cottage projects, re-modeling houses and interior designs, drawing him towards craftspeople, drawing him to local materials and drawing him into the limited techniques and methods of a native vernacular.

In this microcosm he learned of stone walls, tiled roofs, wood beams, the countryside landscape and its rustic nuances. He knew to use the courtyards he grew up in as 'enclosing spaces' and not as rubber stamped 'ethnic architecture.' He imagined 'floating through spaces,' and 'sailing across surfaces'; he invented objects looking at one another, rather than engaging each other in some theoretical preconceived, superficially contrived paradigm. In Patil's work there are no articulated, velvet boxes copied from Europe, blemishing his repertoire of thoughts. There are no paramodern clichés yelling and screaming.

This struggle between freedom of imagination and disruptive imagineering, is where the Indian mindset struggles; each one of us is situated somewhere along the influence line between the molten core and the blissful edge.

The core is beckoning us like an imaginary beautiful siren; calling out to us to migrate, tempting us to copy, asking us to do advanced foreign degrees, and luring us to jump into the fire of no return, perhaps surviving it all in some remote Texas suburb, or in an ethnic neighborhood of Manchester.

Out on the edge there is the music of the wind in leaves and rustling branches; the lullaby of birds singing full throated; the aroma of flowers... real flowers, in full bloom; with the clouds forming vast, lost patterns in the skies; and the satisfaction that one can BE themselves and not SEEM to be what they are not!

Page 10,11: The champa court in the architect's farmhouse.
Left: Built form enveloped by elements of nature at the Sonawane Residence.

Anand Mahindra

HUMAN CENTRIC SPACES

I have always thought that architecture is the most value adding of the arts, (yes, I do believe it is an art form), combining as it does, elegance of form with relevance of function. As a one-time student of architecture, it is one of my greatest pleasures to get involved with the architecture and design of buildings built for the Mahindra Group. And the more I do this, the more I realize what an all pervasive influence architecture can have on our lives, even though we may not always realize it.

Talking about how unaware we are of the influence of communications media on our lives, Marshall McLuhan once said "Whoever discovered water, it wasn't the fish." I think the same holds true of architecture. We are so surrounded by it that we are often oblivious to its existence. We don't stop to think about what it means and what a profound influence it has on our lives, on our behavior and on how we interact with our fellow human beings. And yet so much of what we do is subtly shaped by the architectural environment in which we do it. Architectural design, both reflects a culture as well as creates it. If a culture is focused, left brained, task oriented, valuing the individual over the community, it will give rise to buildings and cities that are built around serried, regimented, logical grids. Conversely, designing such cities or buildings can also create such a culture – think Wall Street or Singapore. On the other hand, if you want to create a city or a work environment that promotes personal and social interaction, or reflects a culture where relaxed community interaction is core, you will avoid sharply delineated, self replicating lay outs. Rather you will design personalised work or living spaces around a common center (a town square, a park or a piazza) that pulls people out of their individual spaces and draws them into the common core – as many Mediterranean cultures, or for that matter, our village chowks do. Architecture probably originally was simply a way to keep humankind safe, warm and sheltered. But today it is far more than that. It is a way to communicate cultural identity and influence human behavior. It symbolizes an approach to work and to life.

Communicating cultural identity and creating human centric spaces is the hall mark of Sanjay Patil's work. What I really appreciate about him is that he sees architecture not as a way to make a living, but as a higher calling. He sees it as a way to harmonise man and nature, the traditional and the contemporary, action and reflection. He sees it as a way to enhance the human spirit and help

it flower. In his work, the indoors flows into the outdoors. Conventional barriers are erased. Light and colour uplift the mood. The beauty of simplicity is captured in the uncluttered lines, in the use of clay and stone and wood. Local materials and craftsmanship are cleverly combined to reflect cultural heritage as well as a modern sensibility. The unity between man and environment is gently underlined. Above all, it is the human being and the welfare of the human being that is at the center of his thought process. I think Sanjay achieves the highest goal that an architect can aspire to – he designs for human happiness.

These virtues find expression in the buildings Sanjay Patil has designed for the Mahindra Group. The Mahindra Management Development Center at Nashik is a place of retreat from everyday pressures. It provides space for calm reflection, for the pursuit of knowledge and the exchange of ideas. The lush green landscape delights the eye and soothes the soul. The classrooms bring people together and set the stage for vigorous intellectual debate. By way of counterpoint, the zen like views and the simple stone benches that strew the paths encourage introspection and informal interaction. The thoughtful design makes it a place where learning and thinking can flower.

The Mahindra Institute of Quality which is next door provides complementarity as well as contrast. It retains the simplicity and environmental harmony of MMDC. There is visual and stylistic continuity. Yet through the use of bold geometric lines, colours and forms, it projects an entirely different character, more in keeping with a training institute where technical skills are the focus. It is a tribute to Sanjay's skills that both these buildings, so different in character, retain their individuality, and yet form part of one seamless whole.

Winston Churchill once said "We shape our buildings; thereafter they shape us." That is a profound truth that Sanjay Patil has fully incorporated in his work. At the Mahindra Group, his buildings will continue to shape us, for a long time to come.

Left: A pause point in the architect's workplace, Environ Planners.

Anurag Kashyap

THE VALUES TO ADORE...

'What is good architecture all about?'

Probably the most difficult question to answer and many of us may have our own perceptions about it. For holding the leader's position at an architectural institute, facing this question beyond personal interpretation becomes inevitable. Thus the answer from my end carries a responsibility for representing the sacred platform that has a great power to influence thousands of young minds as aspiring professionals that eventually has a significant impact on the future of the profession.

I always believed that architectural education cannot be confined to the four walls of classrooms...rather it's a living experience, where the entire life serves as an educator. In this ever changing world, we recognize the need for students of architecture to work collaboratively in multi cultural environment. Building a new venture based on this philosophy, BNCA stretches its arms towards ever-widening thought and action for architectural education through community participation. We firmly believe that Institutes do not make society rather stand as its reflection.

Institutes also share the responsibility to serve

Page 16,17: Levels and pathways at Kusumagraj Memorial.
Right: Wall mural at the Bakshi House.

the role of bridging the gap between academics, profession and society; connectors between ideal and real; between theory and practice.

Thus they cannot work as islands rather they are like a microcosm, well connected to their communities. By saying this, when an institute supports any philosophy or considers some practices worth appreciating, it is likely to be considered as a plural voice that underlines a wider and rational acceptance.

As they say, 'Giving roots of responsibilities and wings of freedom' is precisely expected and thus setting right examples in this premise becomes all the more crucial task.

With this at the backdrop, I take pride to narrate a story that gives an insight on some set of values to adore and a vision to nurture.

In the year 1980, a young professional gets honoured with a degree from Sir J.J. School of Architecture, Mumbai; one of the most renowned institute of that time and of great dignity at national and international platform.

It was the time when awareness of architecture as profession was nascent in India and the practicing professionals very few in number. It was likely that most of them were aspiring to set their ambitions in various ways such as to perceive higher education through a Masters course, working for mentors, handling some good scale projects with multinational companies, or at least set up a firm in a metro city where the scope would be of wider application. This graduated architect, surprisingly, choose a different path that was laid towards his roots in the small city of Nashik.

Courageous it sounds...! As such cities were not really proficient in architectural vocabulary. The city was now blessed with an opportunity to gain a new identity with elevated standards for its image. His passion for architecture took over a plight on the minds of city dwellers and soon his works became a benchmark for the city's evolving built character.

His approach brings life to the structures by integrating context and vernacular values to the living spaces where nature finds its own room and a new home to live in. Spatial

Left: Alternating repetition of lines create shading devices at the N.D.M.V.P.S.' College of Engineering campus.

planning with due consideration to the dweller's needs and thoughtful use of local material reinforces the 'regionalised' feel of spaces and gives a sense of belonging to the user as well as make a strong native bond with the settings.

Vernacular ethos well integrated with contemporary trends give rise to the aesthetics that is further rendered with the graceful collaboration of simplicity and cultural flamboyance.

As a reflection of his personality the qualities such as truth, honesty, simplicity, maturity, stands as a bold expression through his crafted spaces that are more associated to the dwellers and become an inseparable part of their life experience.

With this discussion it is worth mentioning the contribution of two creative personalities for which the city is already known; the great wordsmith, poet Kusumagraj and Dadasaheb Phalke, the pioneer of film industry in India . Inspiring architectural creations emerged through the works of this great architect adds up another chapter to the glory of this blessed city.

Minaz Ansari

IN HIS WORDS

Right: Exploring history and architecture at the Laling Fort near Dhulia, Maharashtra

Sanjay Patil is a man of few words. Complex theories are outside of his comfort zone. He is a person who seldom speaks about his philosophy towards architecture and life. His perspectives can be best observed through his work and his day to day life. Architecture is his strongest communication link to the rest of the world and how? Walk into any of his designs and one can build a dialogue with the spaces he crafts, which compel you to stop and wonder – Who is Sanjay Patil? What drives him to consistently come up with architecture that stimulates the mind and comforts the soul?

To find answers to these and many other questions we follow Sanjay Patil to his weekend office, where he unwinds and energises himself in its natural milieu. Hoping that the tranquil surroundings will help him open up, we start a dialogue with the architect and unravel his story in his own words...

"Nasik is my most loved place." He says. "Its culture, climate, the Godavari and the transformation of the city over the decades is very much a part of me. I was born and brought up in Nashik and I enjoyed my childhood here. My school vacations were spent at my maternal grandfather's house in the village, which gave me my first exposure to well designed, climate responsive design, which responds to summers and winters alike."

"How did architecture happen? Any lasting impressions of student life?" I probe.

"I was fascinated with architecture because it dealt with both science as well as the arts. I gave a serious thought to medicine and engineering, but soon realized that it is not my cup of tea. I was fortunate to get one of the last seats to the J. J. School of Architecture in Mumbai. For a small town boy from a vernacular medium, adjusting to the cosmopolitan culture of a metropolis was overwhelming. So I first became an observer and found friends in other boys like me. The environment at the campus was brilliant. The culture promoted transparency and learning between the various disciplines that existed there. Interaction with my seniors helped me open up. Also, we had very inspiring faculty members who were passionate about their role

Above: A quiet moment in nature's embrace at the Sandan Valley Trek.

as teachers.

Mumbai introduced us to different communities, religions, languages and enriched my personality to a large extent. I wanted to spend some time working with the stalwarts in the industry there before I came back to Nashik. But my average marks ensured that I was not selected and so I promptly returned home. After working in an architectural firm for a few months, I started out on my own. Architecture was not a well recognised profession back then in Nashik, so initial projects started with small houses and other projects for family and friends."

"It's been over three decades since then." I remark, bringing him back to the present. "Looking back, what is it that you think has fascinated you about architecture all along?"

"Everything!" he says, "Architecture to me is not a mere profession; to me it's a passion, a reflection of myself. It is also a process of understanding context, climate, culture and most importantly, the user. The process of seeing a building take form gives me an

Above: A great time of interaction, informal discussions and learning with Ar. B. V. Doshi on his visit to the architect's farmhouse at Mahirvani

adrenaline rush. The continued satisfaction derived by the user is its greatest reward.

Over the years I have found that one should not perceive architectural practice as merely a profit and loss statement. The gains are immense and they come from enjoying the process of evolution of the project, including the labour pains that come with it. One can infuse a soul into the design only by deep-rooted passion for work. The courage to experiment leads to unexpected answers. The sheer pleasure that comes from a job well done makes every effort worthwhile. After all, success is about doing what you love and loving what you do."

"What makes you choose certain projects?" I ask, "And how much influence does the client have on the design?"

"I have never strived to choose my work. Every project that comes to me is equally important. It is very essential to understand a client's dreams and aspiration for the project. I always try to incorporate it in the solution. It often gives me the cue to the design. When certain things are not feasible they can be easily explained with logic. I have been fortunate to have very supportive clients who are open to ideas. In fact, a lot of my learning has come from them. Today most of them are close friends, which for me means a huge accomplishment in life."

A dragonfly hums lazily across the palm trees in the courtyard steering our conversation towards his love for nature.

"Nature has been my consistent teacher. Humility, adaptability and resilience are amongst the few lessons that one can learn from nature. I have grown up enjoying nature and even today I love being a part of it, admiring its forms and variety. My quest for being one with nature is what urges me to go trekking so often. All my designs respect existing natural features and include nature as part of the solution."

"So, what besides trekking are your interests in life and how do they influence architecture?"I probe further.

"I have always been a keen follower of various art forms; specifically Hindustani classical music, theater and poetry. The rhythm, scale and poetry in music have at some level subconsciously contributed to the work I produce. Other than this, I enjoy being outdoors, traveling, exploring nature and learning from other architects and their works. From the start of my career, we like-minded friends formed a group and have travelled to various places across the country and the globe in our search of good architecture. I also enjoy capturing these moments on my camera;

Left: An opportunity of rediscovering the streets of old Nashik with Late Ar. Charles Correa and colleagues.

buildings, glimpses of nature and people.

The major influences from my travel have been the works of master architects B. V. Doshi, Charles Correa, Geoffery Bawa and Tadao Ando to name a few. Travel helps one explore the context in which different buildings have been designed. What really fascinates me is the scale and spatial quality of a building which defines the spirit of the space; construction technology and materials may differ.

I have also always been keen on sharing my experiences or any new information with others. For many years I was involved in formal teaching and I remember that period as a learning process for myself. It also improved my reading a lot. In our office, knowledge sharing is an integral part of gaining it. We regularly hold seminars and interactive sessions in our office amphitheater with people from various fields. And yes, these forums are open to anybody who's interested."

I gently steer him to more deep-seated questions about himself and his passion. "Is there a strong philosophy that you would want to reflect in your designs? How do you conceive a project?"

"I may disappoint you in saying that I have never really followed or tried to project any fixed philosophy. Maybe it stems from the fact that I have never trained under anyone. I am always open to different concepts and ideologies. As long as it serves the purpose of the design, no approach, no material is wrong. I make no claims to be gifted with immense creativity. Whatever I know, I have learnt from my surroundings, the traditional spaces I grew up in, from nature and people around me. And to me learning is a never ending process. One must never give up one's curiosity for discovering new things in life.

Architecture to me is this process of evolution and day to day improvisation. There is no instant answer, at least in my case. A logical analysis of the site along with climate and respect for nature and the land it's built on, usually provides most of the answers. I start my day early morning with site visits that help me evaluate the project and evolve finer details. As I have often said, the design process is never complete till every aspect of the design runs through one's blood stream. Good quality of natural light and ventilation, sustainability and infusion of nature has been constant in every design, whereas form and material vary."

The brutal honest response urges me to my next question "So what does design really mean to you?"

"Design is a reflection of one's true nature. I am a very simple, straightforward person and hence I find it very difficult to develop complex designs. My approach therefore is towards evolving simple, truthful spaces. It comes naturally to me. The same approach helps me select materials that are very basic and detailing which is easy and minimalist. My intention is always to make the user happy by meeting his needs and aspirations. I have never really thought beyond that.

For me design is also a collaborative process. The involvement of craftsman from the start, other team members in the office is very important to this process. I have always received valuable feedback from my wife Vijaya, who has been my sounding board throughout. Today my daughters give me their blunt, frank opinion which only serves as constructive criticism and adds value to the design.

"So how did this book come about? What is the message that it conveys to the reader?" I ask.

"I was a bit skeptical about publishing my works initially. I never really thought of my work as being so remarkable. The idea of the book finally appealed to me when I saw it as an opportunity to present the journey of a person whose life has been led by his passion. The clear message that I would give to every reader would be to discover one's passion in life and follow it."

"Where do you see this architectural journey taking you in the future?," I wonder aloud.

"I think the future is about sustainable design." He replies without hesitation. "We have always had a strong inclination towards climate responsive design. However, so far our approach has been more based on experience and observation. But now we need to develop a more scientific, methodical approach to sustainable architecture.

We architects often have good intent but shy away from analysis and quantification of things

like solar radiation, wind, sun angles across the year. That needs to change. Sustainability needs to seep into every level of the design. We need to know exactly how a building will perform in relation to climate and comfort. I am also in the process of learning this route to design but the primary need is to accept that sustainable design is no longer an option, but the primary basis of good design."

I finally wrap up my questions and look around at the quaint farmhouse where nature wanders unhindered. Perhaps even today, the tranquillity and warmth that the space exudes has been a catalyst in coaxing this story out of the otherwise elusive Sanjay Patil; a fine illustration of how even the designer cannot escape the effects of the positive vibes of the spaces he creates.

Above: Contemplating life through architecture with Ar Christopher Charles Benninger at the architect's farmhouse, Mahirvani.

COURTYARDS WHICH LIVE

An early morning walk along the streets of old Nashik introduces you to some elements which define the architectural vocabulary of this mystical old town - the serene ghats of the Godavari, narrow shaded streets meandering meaningfully towards it and the traditional wada houses lining these streets.

The housing typology of old Nashik is defined by these wadas and a detailed study of the vernacular architecture around the old city reveals certain governing design principles that have unknowingly been reflected in the architecture across the region over a period of time. These principles were drawn out of respect for nature, a response to the local materials and climatic constraints of the region and the cultural and social needs of the inhabitants. Use of locally available building material was a given, at an age and time when transportation of material had its limitations. Louvered windows, shading devices and roof overhangs to shade the surfaces are commonly observed as the structure's defences against the travails of nature.

Courtyards have been an integral part of these wadas, serving as an important and multifunctional common space at the heart of the structure. Courtyards also responded to the climatic need for convective cooling, to reduce the dry heat characteristic of the region. In addition to courtyards, verandahs and other forms of semi-covered spaces extensively feature in the vernacular houses around the region. They served as spaces to work, sleep, relax and entertain depending on the time of day and year.

In the early eighties, in this very town, a small revolution was being kindled by architect Sanjay Patil, then a fresh graduate from the JJ School of Architecture. Armed with a design philosophy guided by respect for local architecture and love for nature, he set up a practice which led him to experiment and successfully adapt his learning from the historic city that he grew up in. A sustainable approach to architecture formed an important aspect of his practice decades before it became a buzzword globally.

One of the major milestones which reinforced this philosophy was a self-prompted documentation exercise of a wada at Vinchur in Nashik district in the year 1982. The days and nights spent living in and measuring the space, helped explore every minute aspect of the spatial quality, planning and detailing of the house and further reinforced the values that vernacular architecture is associated with.

The first reflection of his influences and architectural philosophy is the Deshmukh House

Left: Deep vernadas at the Vinchur wada.

in Nashik, completed in 1990. This was one of the earliest courtyard houses designed by the architect. The essence of wada houses typical to this region and climate is brought about by the simplicity and openness of the plan. The use of traditional materials like timber, in-situ flooring and Mangalore tiles further reinforces the effect. The open to sky courtyard forms the visual, spatial and social focal point and brings in all the elements of nature into the house. Repetition of form by use of arches around the courtyard creates an invisible screen around it. It also gives an intimate scale to the space.

After some initial designs which interpreted the traditional courtyard in the present day context, the architect began developing variations of the same. The challenge lay in blending age old concepts to suit modern sensibilities and lifestyles. A noteworthy example of this is the Parmeshwaran House built in1994.

The design of this house moved away from the traditional colonnaded courtyard by eliminating columns around it. This resulted in a seamless flow of space from the covered to the uncovered. The living, dining and family seating are linked by one common courtyard. Thus this courtyard forms the geometric and functional centre of the single-storied house. Also, the scale of the courtyard was

From top to bottom:
Team 'Environ Planners' during the documentation exercise of wada at Vinchur.

The colonnaded courtyard in the Deshmukh House.

Traditional influences seen in the sloping roofs and the central courtyard in the Deshmukh House.

A courtyard with traditional elements at the Thakkar House.

From top to bottom:
The column-free courtyard in the Parmeshwaran House.

The entrance courtyard with the champa tree in the Sarda House.

The courtyard breaks the grid and enters into the activity spaces in the Bakshi House.

A private courtyard abutting the bedroom in the Rasne House.

changed to adapt to the scale and needs of a nuclear home.

By the mid-nineties Sanjay Patil's connect with courtyards was growing deeper. His projects were gaining acceptance and visibility and clients were willing to accept a traditional concept remodeled in a new style. To protect them from elements like rodents and mosquitoes and cater to the security needs of modern times, some courtyards were covered with skylights. The detailing of the skylight provided for a clerestory creating a stack effect and enhancing convective cooling in a manner that traditional courtyards did.

The next big step in the development of this concept was the use of multiple courtyards in a single house. A very interesting study in this typology is the Sarda House built in 1996. This sprawling property is occupied by a large joint family spanning three generations. The design is a bold and modern interpretation of a traditional wada by the use of two cuboids juxtaposed into each other, deeply interlocked by multiple courtyards within the space.

Around the turn of the millennium, another noteworthy variant of the multiple courtyard house emerged in the form of the Thakkar House. In this design, the journey of courtyards increased in intimacy, as it penetrated further into the private spaces of the house. The architectural vocabulary of this house however is diverse and rustic as compared to the Sarda House. The sprawling ground floor house is bound together by the multiple courtyards generating a feeling of togetherness. Tiny skylit courtyards became a part of bedrooms and toilets.

By now courtyards had become a second identity of the architect's design philosophy. Sprawling, landscaped pockets of open to sky spaces found a place in other building types such as institutes, office spaces and even factory buildings. The concept further evolved in the design of the Bakshi House. Located along a busy commercial street, the spaces in this residence essentially needed to be inward looking in order to maintain privacy and reduce street noise. A radical design approach was thus devised.

Designed as a composition of large bare planes, articulated with projections and voids, this structure is almost devoid of openings. The spaces within are largely lit by two sprawling courtyard spaces. The living areas are extensions of these courtyards and the private spaces had windows opening into them. An open staircase emerges from within the courtyard making the journey a pleasant experience every time.

In this design the courtyard assumes organic forms to penetrate into the activity areas, blurring the line between the built and the unbuilt. Furniture elements are designed to suit the flow of the courtyard into the living areas. Drenched in skylight and yet isolated from the noisy surroundings, this house essentially revolves around these two breathing pockets.

In the years to come, several houses were bestowed with these blessings of the sky with interesting variations. While the central courtyard in the Rathi House creates a strong centre and uninterrupted connections between the living and dining space, the strategically positioned prayer space within the courtyard in the Kazi House makes spirituality a soothing experience.

A study of these and the many other courtyards designed by the architect really makes one realize how this one space can have such myriad interpretations, so much versatility in terms of use and so much adaptability to the climate, culture and social needs. This little connection between a piece of the sky and a patch of earth truly eases out the stresses of urban life and calms the mind, infusing light and life into an otherwise mundane day. And that is exactly why these have been aptly classified as 'Courtyards which Live'.

Left: A prayer space along the courtyard in the Kazi House.
Page 36,37: Roof overhangs enhance the curvilinear form.

VISUAL CONTEXT

Distribution of projects in the city

The Masani farmhouse was built in the year 1860, a humble abode of a farmer. It then went on to become the ancestral home of the Masani family in 1916. The building continued in the state it was in, until the year 1984 when the clients approached the architect to restore it. Having housed many generations of the family, every part of the house was steeped in memories. On the other hand, having weathered the severities of time and changing seasons for a long period had deteriorated the structure.

The biggest challenge faced by the architect was to accommodate the needs of the day without destroying the existing character of the house. The fundamental design approach to this challenge was established by being true to the existing structure.

The client fortunately had an upbringing that made him sensitive enough to understand the need to restore the space, as against popular opinion of pulling it down and building a new one. Being the son of India's leading timber engineer ensured that his childhood was heavily influenced by the beauty of timber structures. Also a stint in England and exposure to the architectural heritage of the country further reinforced the importance of restoration.

Top: The rustic living room retains its old charm.

Left: The original structure as in 1984.
Right: The house after restoration.

The architect, then a fresh graduate was completely in sync with this philosophy and was more than willing to share ideas and communicate with the client. Armed with a drawing board and drafting instruments, the architect frequented the site on his motorcycle and immersed himself into the process. The expertise of a skilled carpenter at site and a deep involvement and tuning with the client helped the design evolve.

In the restored farm house, the structural grid has been retained with additional rooms like a modern kitchen, toilet and verandas being wrapped around the existing spaces.
The workspaces are located at the rear, with the living areas fronting the house. An on-site discovery of an existing connection between the two levels led to the creation of a vertical communication within the house.

The attic on the uppermost level has been converted into a cosy children's room by adding a dormer roof. Balconies on the east and west open out into natural breeze and the massive pitched roof shelters the spaces below. The veranda enveloping the lower floor has been treated with thick walls and arched openings to create a shaded transitional space between the private spaces indoors and the outside world.

The existing wooden floors were stripped of old layers of paint and treated to reveal the natural character of the material. The floor cavity has been effectively used for running electrical and plumbing lines. Existing niches, pegs and other rustic details have been restored. In situ mosaic flooring feels cool and inviting under bare feet and rough cast plaster adds to the rustic feel.

Water from the existing reservoir has been used to create a swimming pool outside the house. The water from the pool is in turn used for irrigation in the adjoining fields thereby eliminating the need of a filtration plant. Respect for the existing structure and a sincere attempt to retain its character infuses positivity and balance in the design. Sensitive details echo the times gone by; as even today every space in the farmhouse narrates a story from its memoirs.

Left: Deep verandas added to create a shaded transitional space.

Left: Vertical connections with the upper level.
Right: The original wooden members restored to the natural look after stripping off layers of paint.

Left: A series of arched openings created around the veranda.
Right: The existing structure merges seamlessly with the new.

SECTION - AA'

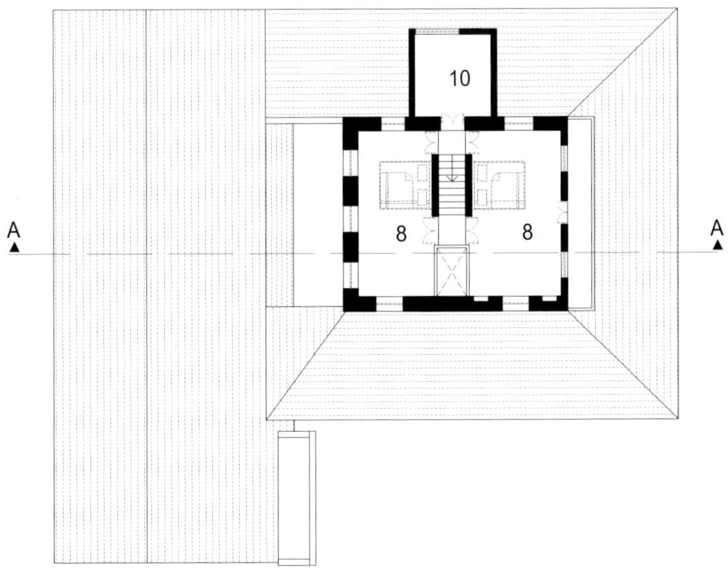

FIRST FLOOR PLAN

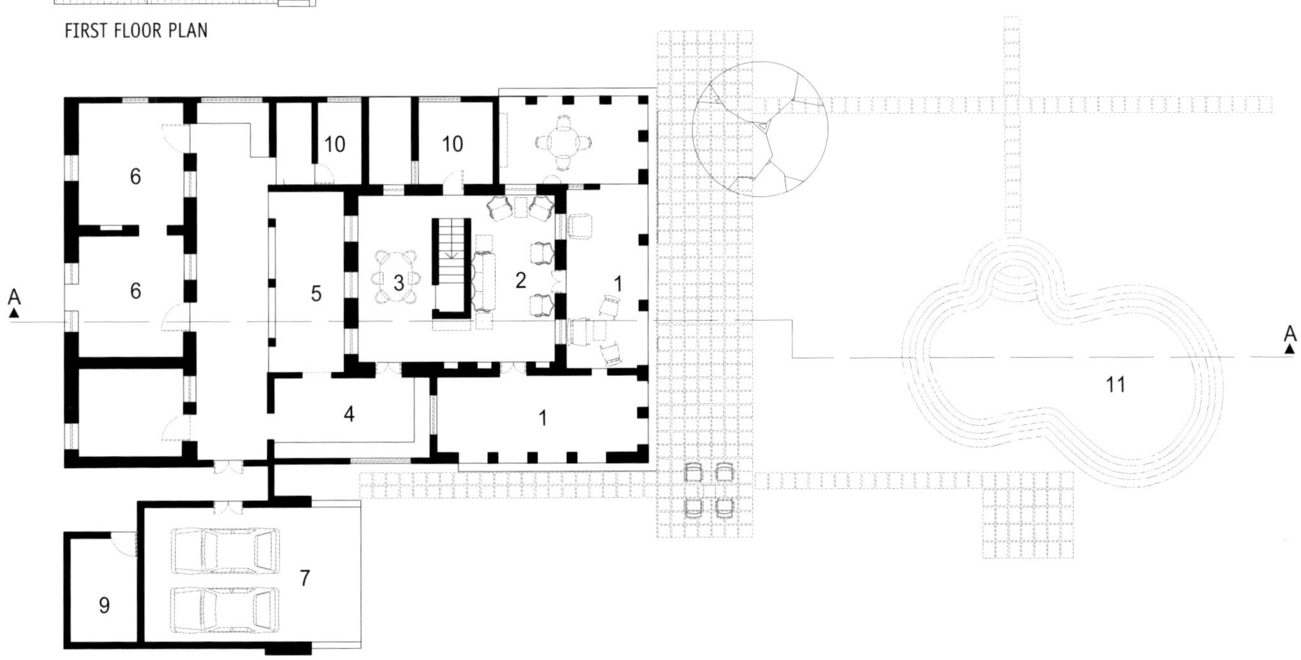

GROUND FLOOR PLAN

1.VERANDA
2.LIVING ROOM
3.DINING ROOM
4.KITCHEN
5.COURTYARD
6.OFFICE
7.GARAGE
8.BEDROOM
9.STORAGE
10.TOILET
11.SWIMMING POOL CUM WATER TANK FOR AGRICULTURAL USE

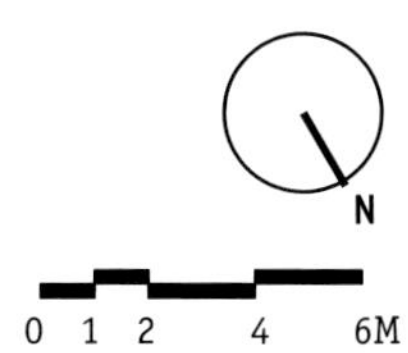

MAHINDRA MANAGEMENT DEVELOPMENT CENTRE

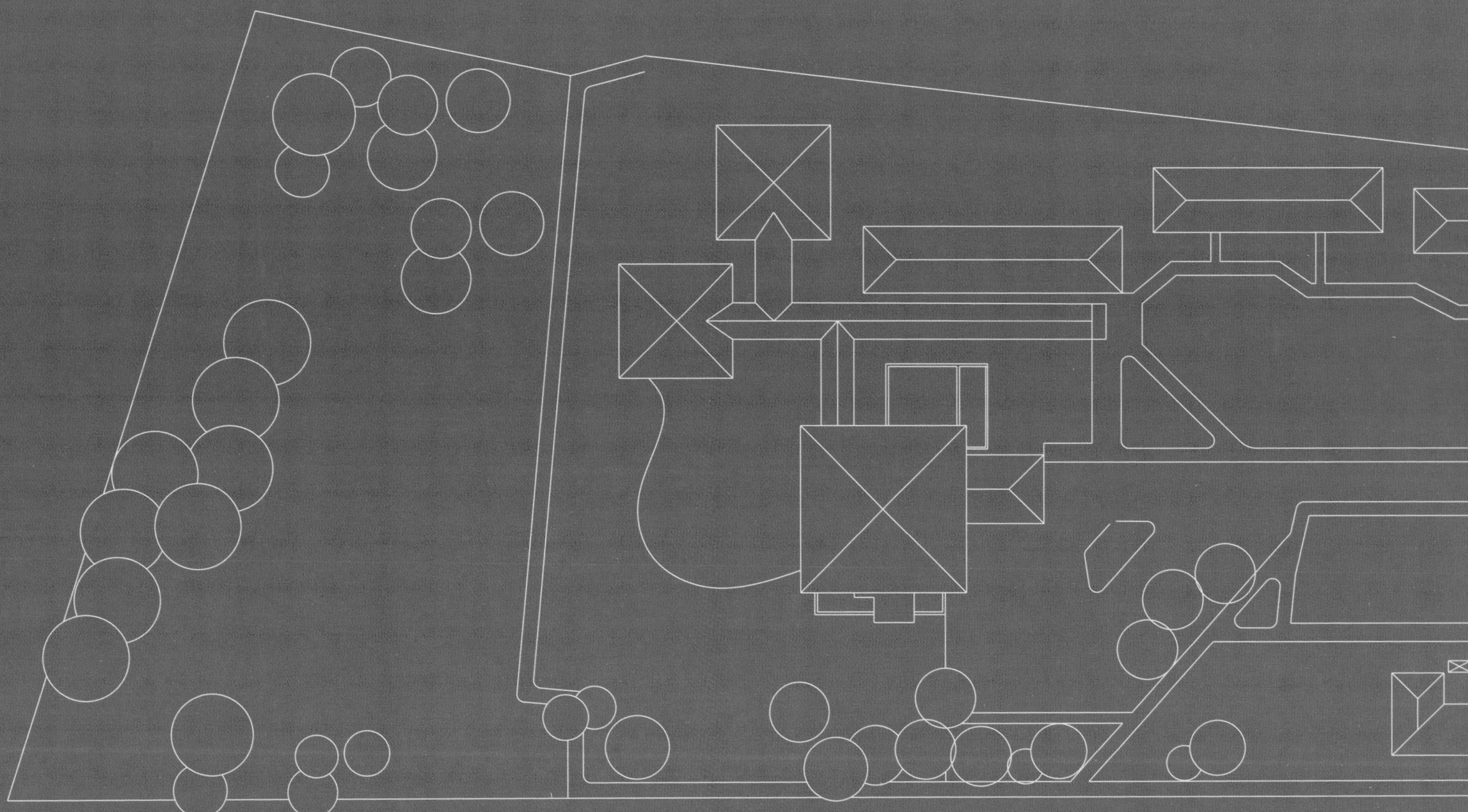

1998

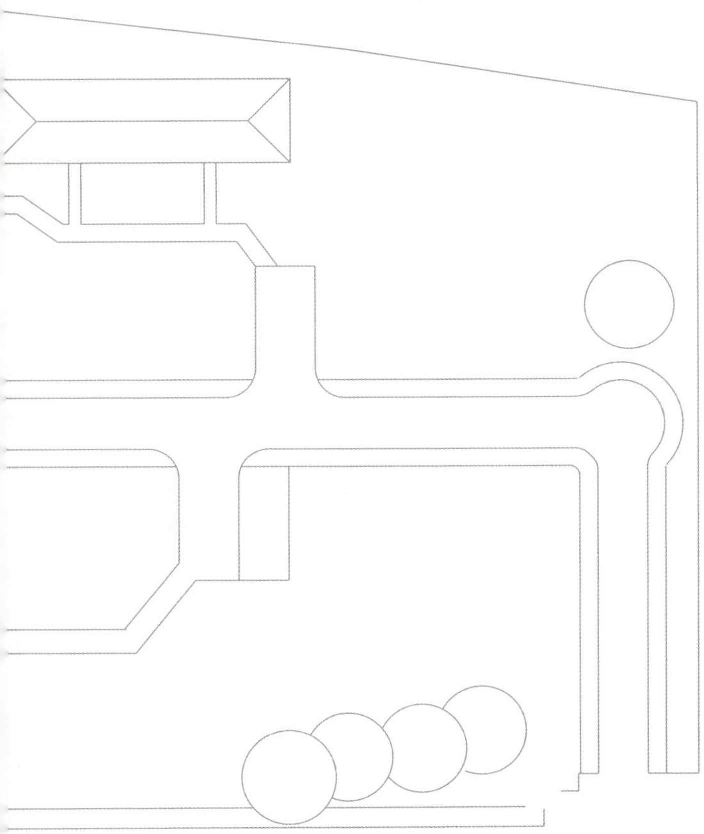

Above :Rhythm created using coursed natural stone.

Learning under a tree has been historically practiced in our culture. As times changed, learning became formalised into institutes and confined to built spaces. Soon nature became an outsider. Given this context, the design approach for the Mahindra Management Development Centre takes some lessons from our past and answers some relevant questions in the affirmative.

'Can corporate training move out of formal spaces and take place in the lap of nature?

Can interaction take place beyond the confines of a board room and spill over into a courtyard?

Can learning happen amongst the chirping of birds outside of a classroom?'

On the fringes of Govardhan village on the outskirts of Nashik, the Mahindra Management Development Centre (MMDC) stands quiet and serene, a cascade of sloping roofs welcoming the visitor into its fold. This centre for employee training, team interaction and learning was originally meant to be a recreation centre for company employees. However, it was the vision of the chairman of Mahindra group of companies Mr Keshub Mahindra during a visit to site, that suggested that the land be put to more positive

Left: A cascade of sloping roofs at the entrance porch and reception block.

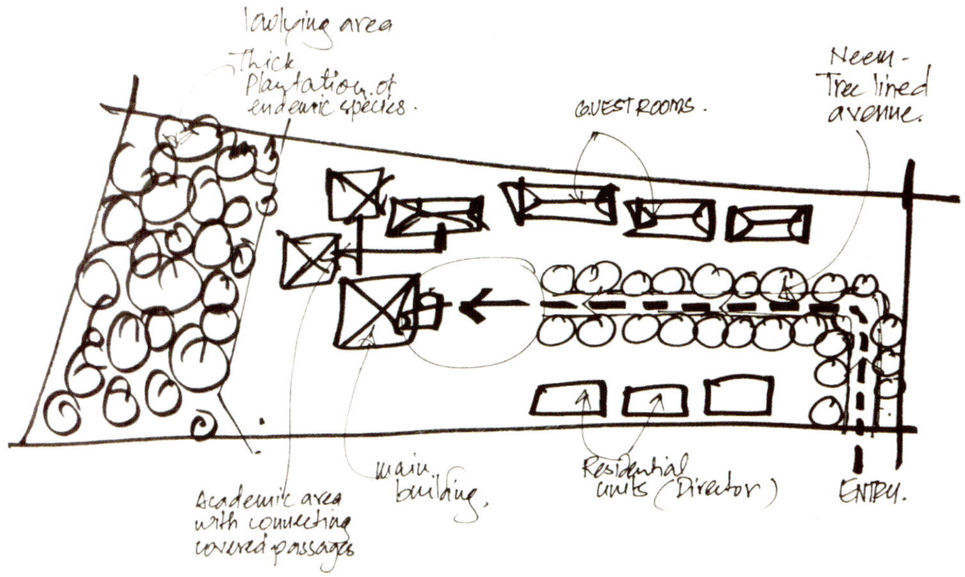

use. The architect sensed the immense potential in the barren low lying piece of land. An approach that blended the contemporary with the vernacular, led to meaningful design.

The entrance lobby has an approach through an avenue of trees that transverse the length of the rectangular parcel of land, lending a fourth dimension to the structure. The main reception welcomes you with its soft yellow stone flooring and its generous volume of space; strong and unfolding column connections holding up the massive sloping roof. The structural steel rafters and circular columns merge effortlessly with the polished wooden roof boards. The clay roof tiles complete the structure and form, embracing the spaces below with their strength and warmth.

This focal space holds the common recreation and dining spaces which logically branch out into paths and goals leading to various seminar and training areas. Square punctures at strategic locations serve as zen views providing glimpses of the greenery beyond. The rustic roughness of the stone and clay is balanced by painted white interiors and state of the art training and conferencing facilities. Users gravitate towards the pause points provided outside these spaces in the form of simple stone benches to hold informal discussions. The residential spaces spread out beyond, bounded by private courtyards or cantilever balconies looking into the lush, barrier free landscape.

The land which was originally barren, today nurtures over fifteen hundred fruit trees endemic to the region, giving it a therapeutic experience of growth, apart from a harvest of the local bounties. Alternative techniques like rain water harvesting, solid waste management and sensor based lighting make the campus sustainable.

Learning at MMDC gives one an opportunity to reach out and become one with nature, proving to be a perfect antidote to the stresses of a busy work life.

Left: Lawn mounds meet stone walls and clay tiled roofs in the learning block.

Left top: Unfolding column connections hold up the massive spans.
Left bottom: The reception lobby with its warm natural stone flooring and generous volume.
Right: Connecting pathways flanked by pockets of green.

Left top: The residential spaces with balconies overlooking the landscape.
Left bottom: Entrance to the guest rooms.

Right top: Entrance through a courtyard to a residential block.
Right bottom: Comfort and warmth envelope the guest rooms.

SECTION - AA'

1.ENTRANCE TO SITE
2.PARKING
3.ADMINISTRATIVE BLOCK
4.DINING
5.CLASS ROOMS
6.GUEST ROOM FOR FACULTY
7.GYMNASIUM
8.RESIDENTIAL ACCOMMODATION
9.EXECUTIVE COTTAGES
10.ORCHARD
11.SERVANT QUARTERS

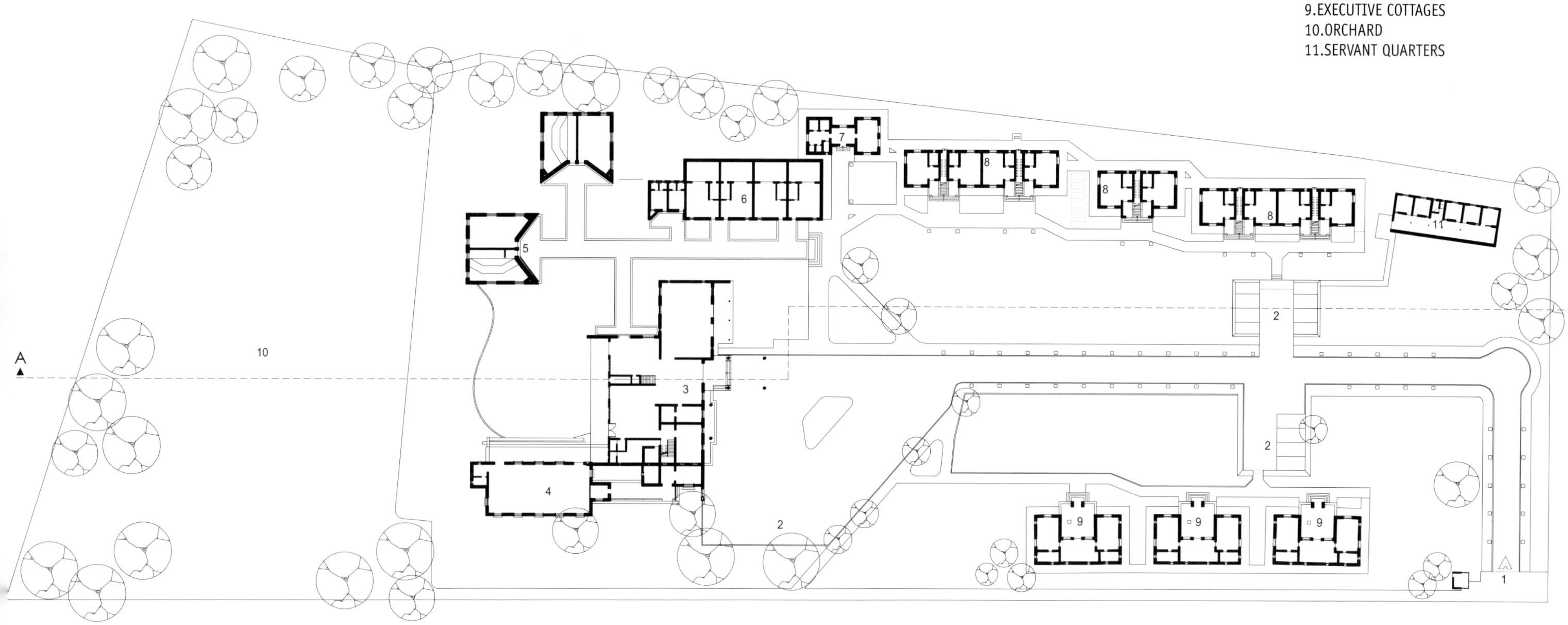

SITE PLAN

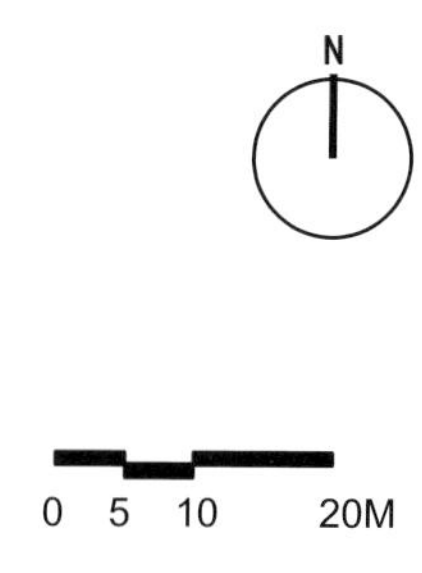

Left: A glimpse of the campus from the residential block.

ARCHITECT'S OWN WORKSPACE

2000

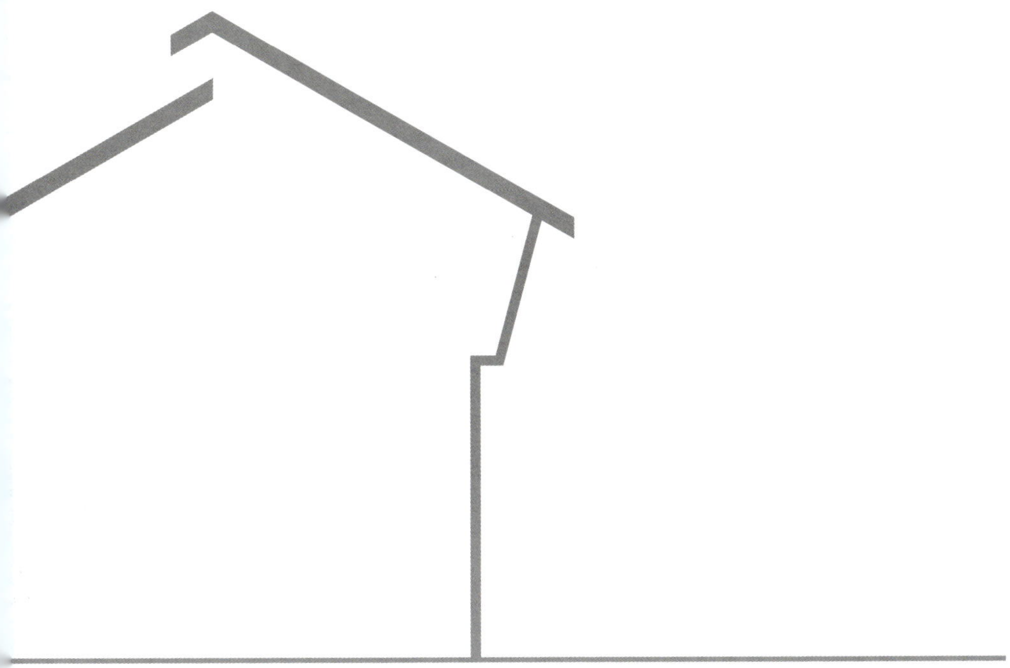

Above: Earth and water elements infuse tranquility.

In a discreet lane in Nashik lies the architect's office. Tucked around a little corner behind a deceptively plain garden wall, away from the hustle bustle of a commercial district, this workspace has many a surprise awaiting you. The entrance steers you in, along a winding brick pathway, flanked by a riot of flowers on either side. Glimpses of the massive pitched roof are visible behind the rising emerald grass mound on the left.

The hide and seek in design continues as one reaches the end of the pathway, with two enticing set of steps luring you alternatively to the reception and the studio. If you choose to enter the reception, the trellised pause point with a simple stone bench awaits you. The office within is simple, flexible and transparent, capable of creating a number of combinations of use within it. The activity pockets in the workspace within are sheltered by the sloping roof combined with the strength of the structural steel that holds up the spans and gives sanctuary to the spaces below.

The upper level of the office merges in, creating an interesting variety in the ceiling heights. Slender slits between spaces and the upper level overlooking the activities below, creates a unity

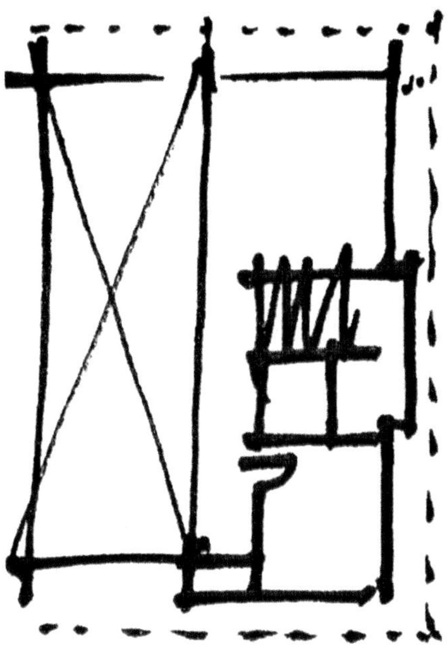

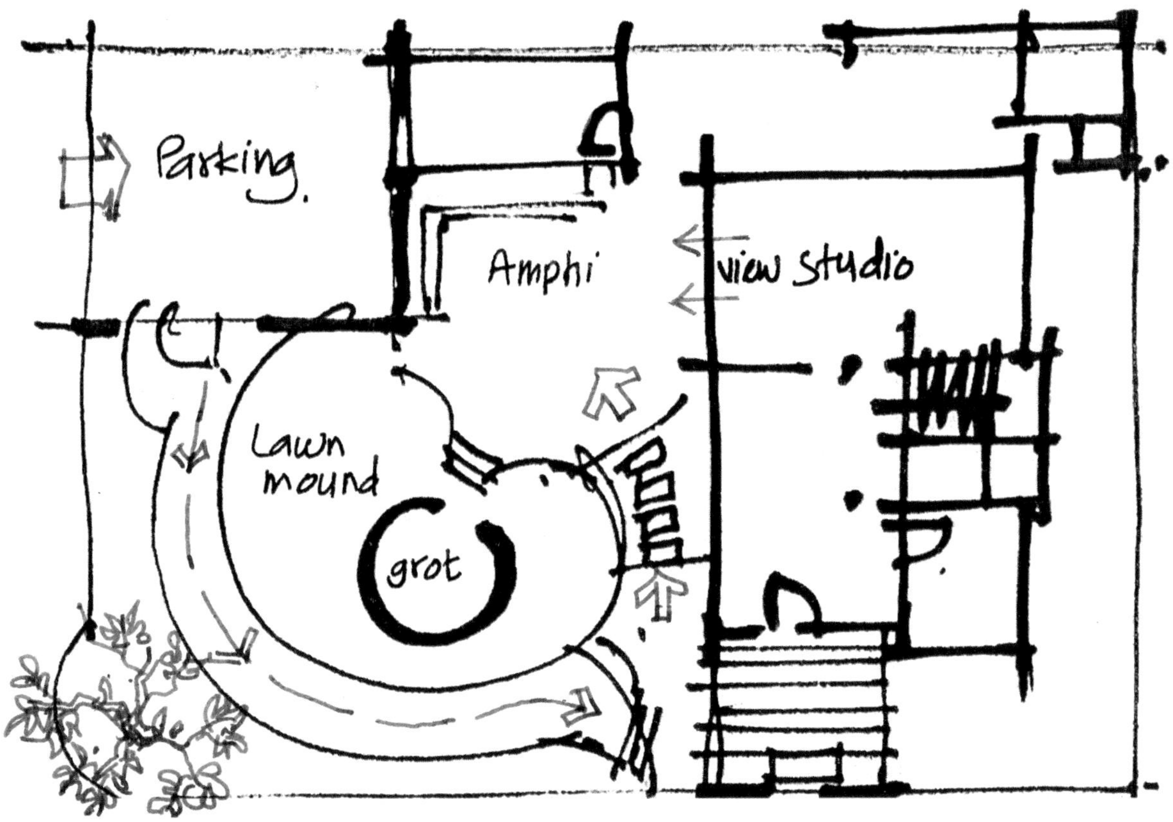

Right top: The brick pathway branching to the reception on the right and the amphitheatre on the left.
Right bottom: The brick paved amphitheatre is a buzzing activity pocket.

between the spaces. The sloping walls of the library with its horizontally pivoted windows fashions out a cosy window seat.

Those who choose to turn to the steps leading to the studio are in for another surprise. Beyond the stepping stones bridging a small water body lays a half hidden garden which is the heart of the office. A brick paved amphitheater and a host of local species of plants, draw you inside and bring nature in your lap.

A quaint pivoted door reveals the secret; well concealed by the mound of green. A ferro-cement dome houses a sanctum of seclusion; an alcove, a gufa, a humble tribute to his mentor Ar Balkrishna Doshi. A single skylight pierces the mound of earth above, bringing in diffused daylight from the north. The swirling patterns on the sides add a splash of colour creating visual drama. In the middle of this bustling workspace one finds an intense solitude and a deep sense of connection to the earth.

For the architect himself, this is the realisation of his long cherished dream which became a reality with perseverance, vision and family support; a personal space to pursue his passion. The word 'office' seems somehow grossly inadequate for this space. This space is a little microcosm in itself, buzzing with activity and infusing one and all with its energy and life. Conversely, it has the tranquillity that compels you to sit down, unwind and retrospect. It is a design lab where ideas are discussed, ideologies are debated and experiments are carried out. And above all it is a metaphor encompassing the philosophy of the architect and a reflection of his personality.

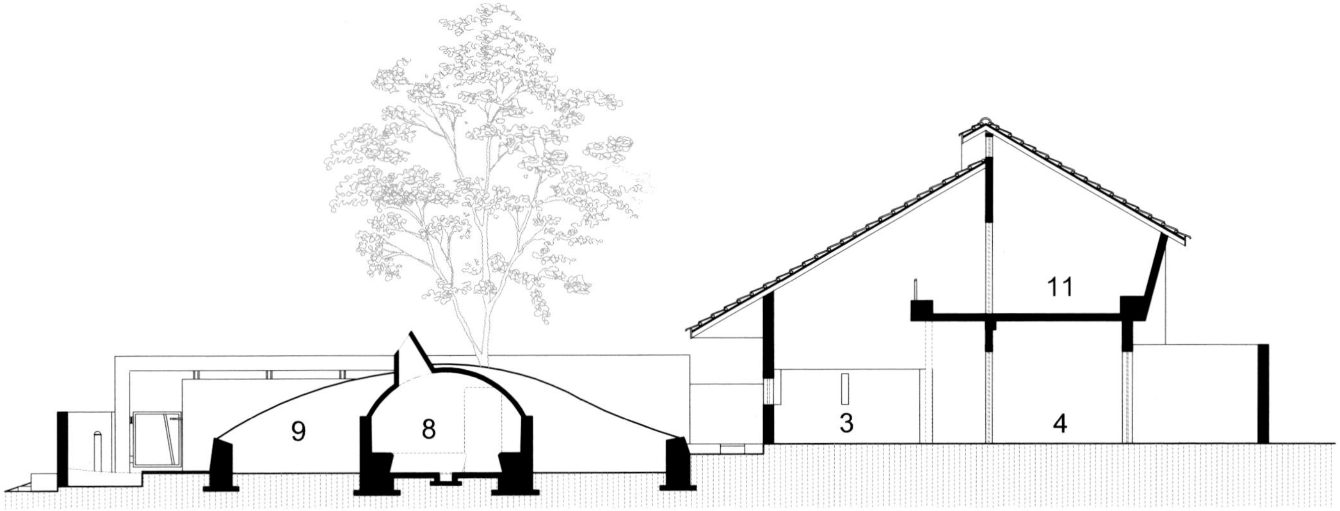

1.PARKING
2.ENTRANCE
3.RECEPTION / WAITING
4.CABIN
5.DISCUSSION ROOM
6.STUDIO
7.AMPHITHEATER
8.GROTTO
9.MOUND
10.LIBRARY + CONFERENCE ROOM
11.REST ROOM
12.STORE

SECTION AA

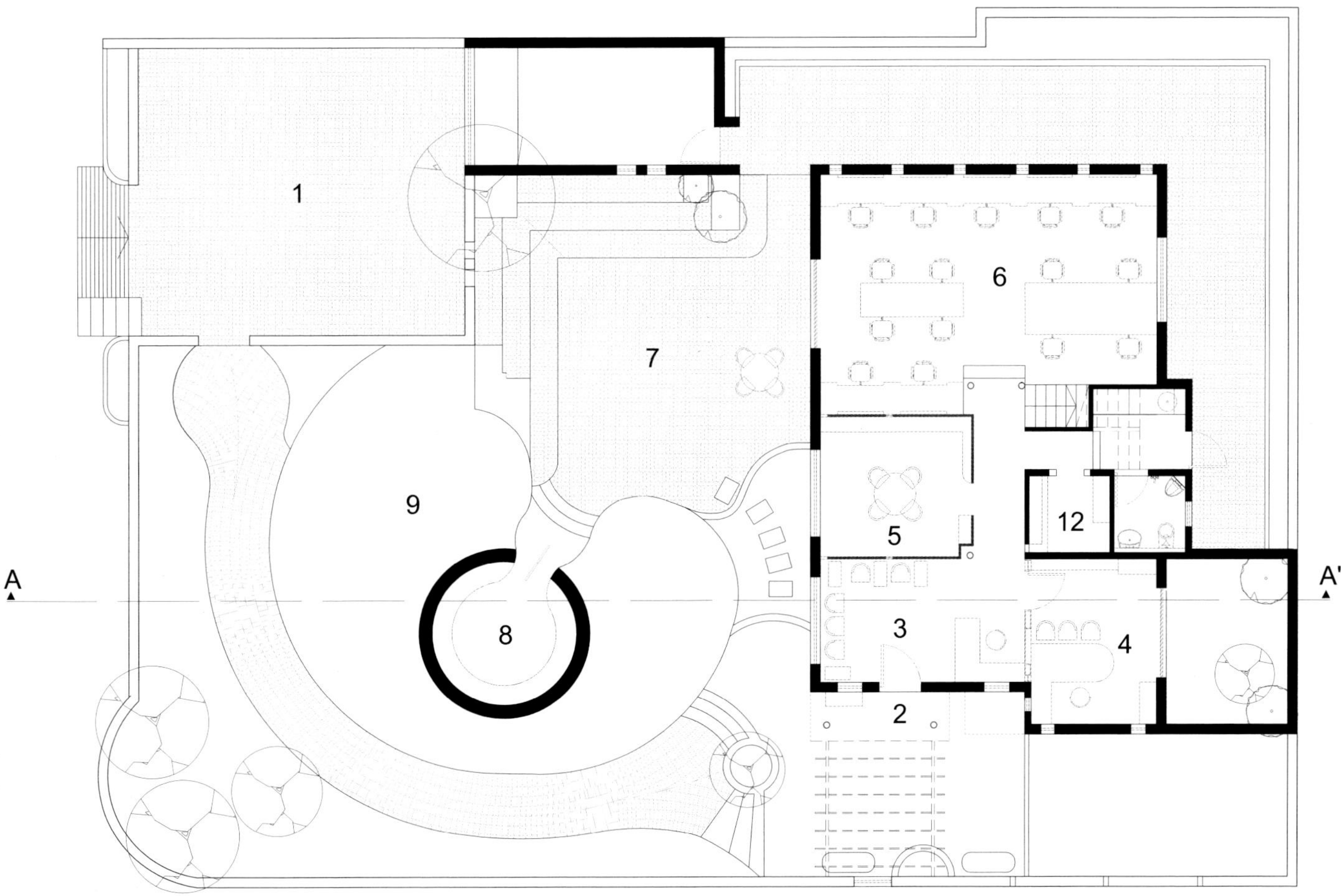

GROUND FLOOR PLAN

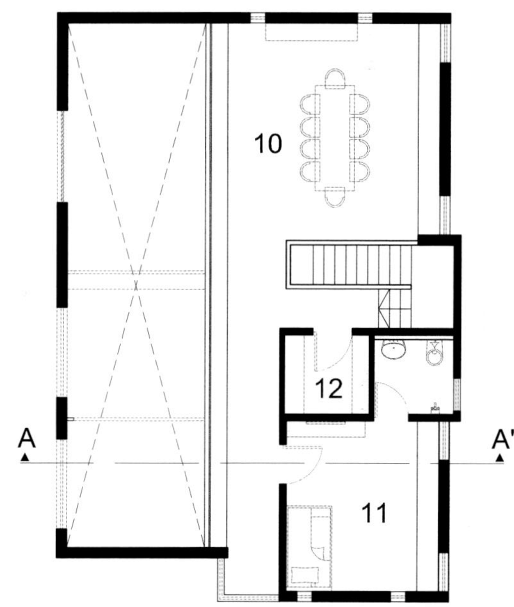

FIRST FLOOR PLAN

Page 64 top: The meeting hub abuts the water body and greenery beyond.
Page 64 bottom: Looking below from the upper level.
Page 65: The half-hidden grotto nestled below a mound of lawn.
Page 66,67: Swirling china mosaic patterns and the conical skylight inside the cave.
Left: Stepping stones give a floating effect over a still water body.

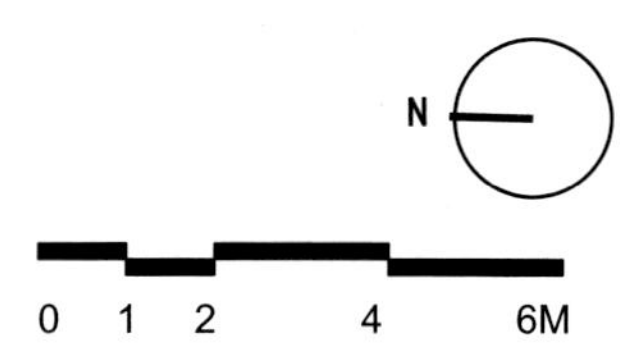

MAHINDRA INSTITUTE OF QUALITY

2003

Above: The language of coursed basalt stone and smooth plastered surface.

Close on the heels of the Mahindra Management and Development Centre (MMDC), Mahindra & Mahindra came up with a requirement for another training facility located in the vicinity of the existing one. This facility proposed to provide technical training programs to its own team members as well as other organizations. These programs are based on the Harvard pattern and designed to be long duration residential ones.

By then, the design vocabulary of MMDC was a strong identification of comfort and character with the users. The challenge for the architect was to create a new identity for the Mahindra Institute of Quality whilst retaining the existing character.

The main training block of the campus was thus developed on a completely new concept.

The training spaces are wrapped around an elliptical landscaped space creating a strong center converging with nature. Bold skewed lines form an amphitheater within, evolving an alternating repetition of lawn and stone paving. The uniformity of this ellipse is broken by the main entrance and lobby space which pierces out of the elliptical block forming an emphatic interlock of volumes.

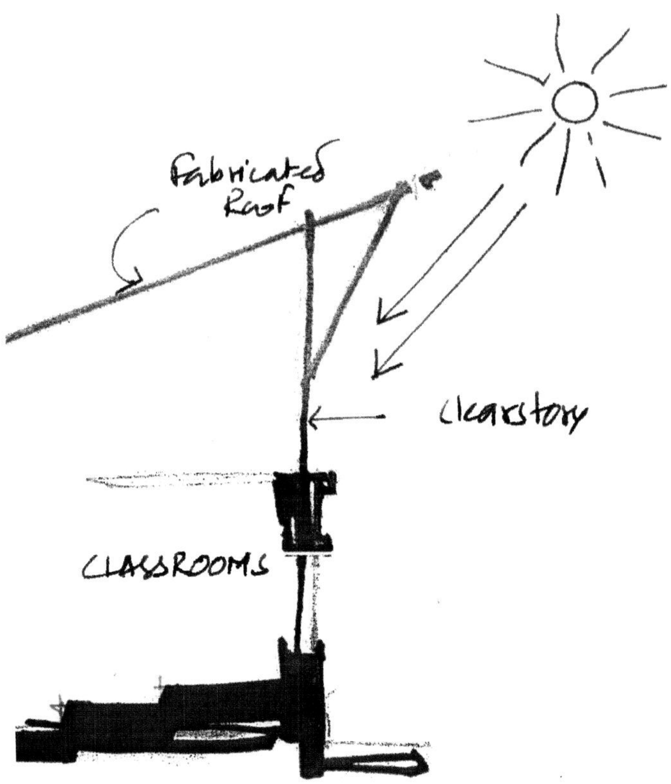

A generous movement area sweeps around the training spaces connecting the indoors to the outdoors. Vertical planes with splashes of colour visually complete the building edge of the elliptical form. Dots, lines and planes are the basic elements used to define the building edge and form patterns in the extensive landscape that binds the campus together. The difference in approach also extends to the landscape which is more geometric in expression and uses exotic plant species as against the organic forms and endemic fruit species used at MMDC.

Pools of light dot the common areas as skylight filters into the space. Open stairs and a connecting bridge scale down the double height space. A generous overhang of the roof creates a strong vocabulary of design around the building, accentuating the curves as well as providing shade. Bands of stone masonry and smooth plaster add rhythm to the form and echo the vocabulary of rustic stone.

Left: The main learning center enjoys a generous foreground.

The residential block reflects the character of mangalore tiled roofs and composite masonry, sit-outs and landscape, yellow jaisalmer stone and cane. The spaces however include clusters of individual rooms connected through a common lounge.

The Mahindra Institute of Quality can be likened in many ways to the gen-next of the earlier facility; rooted in tradition but contemporary in approach. The Mahindra Institute of Quality is modern, different and defiant and yet a chip of the old block from which brand Mahindra was created.

Page 74,75: The main entrance lobby pierces through the elliptical form of the building.
Left top: Rustic warli art embellishes the entrance.
Left bottom: Structural steel roof members and vertical glazing creates a new identity.
Right: Vertical fins with splashes of colour visually complete the elliptical form.

Left top: Structural steel supports designed to hold up the staircase and connecting bridge.
Left bottom: Geometric expressions in landscape using some exotic plant species.
Right: The waiting lounge connects to the central landscape.

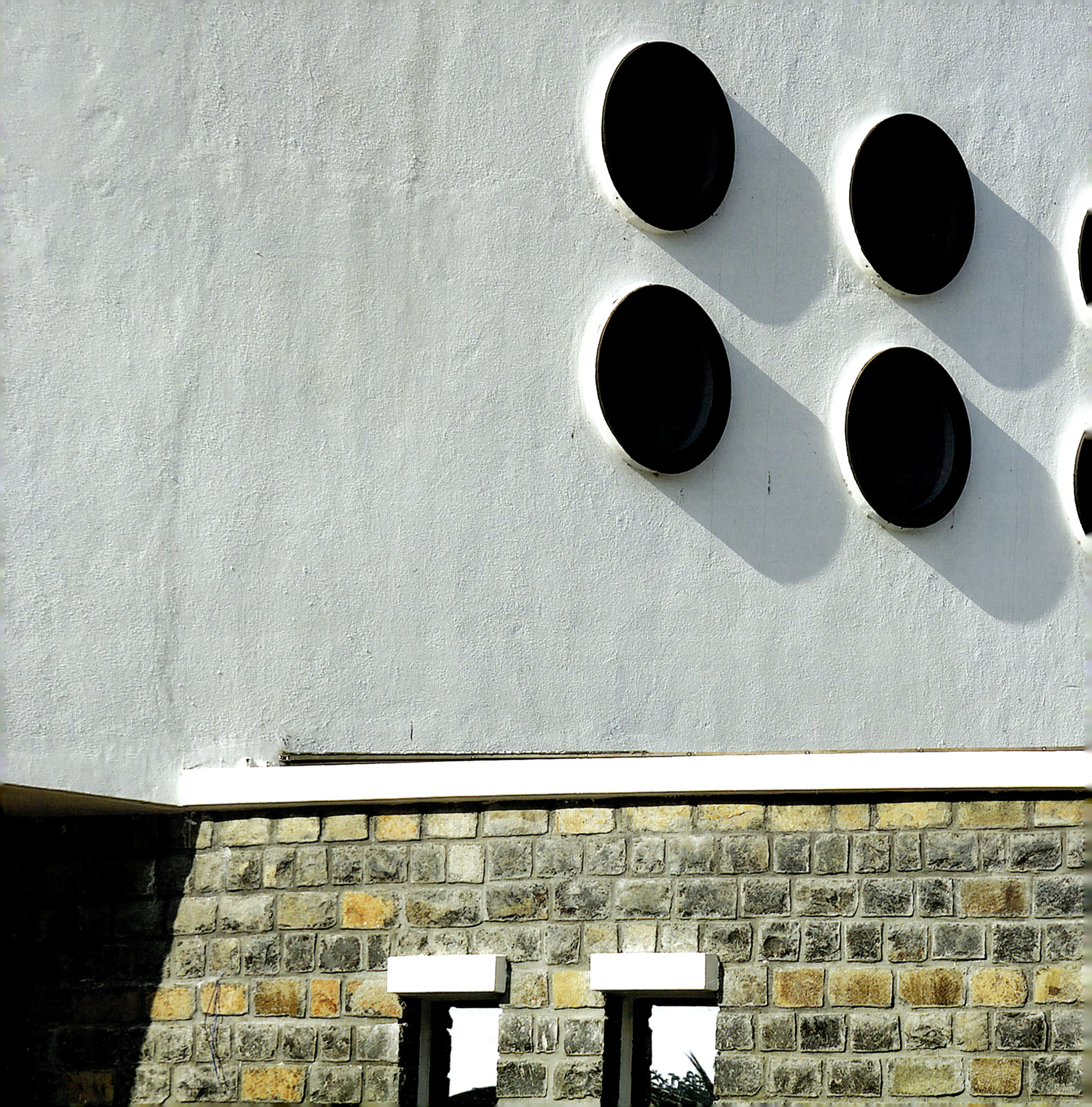

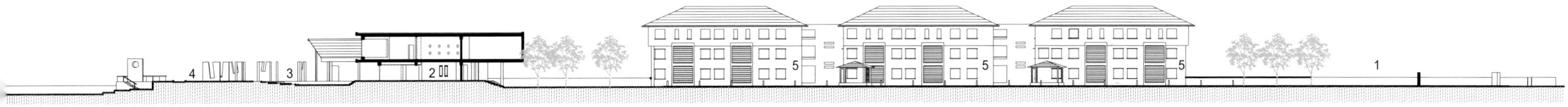

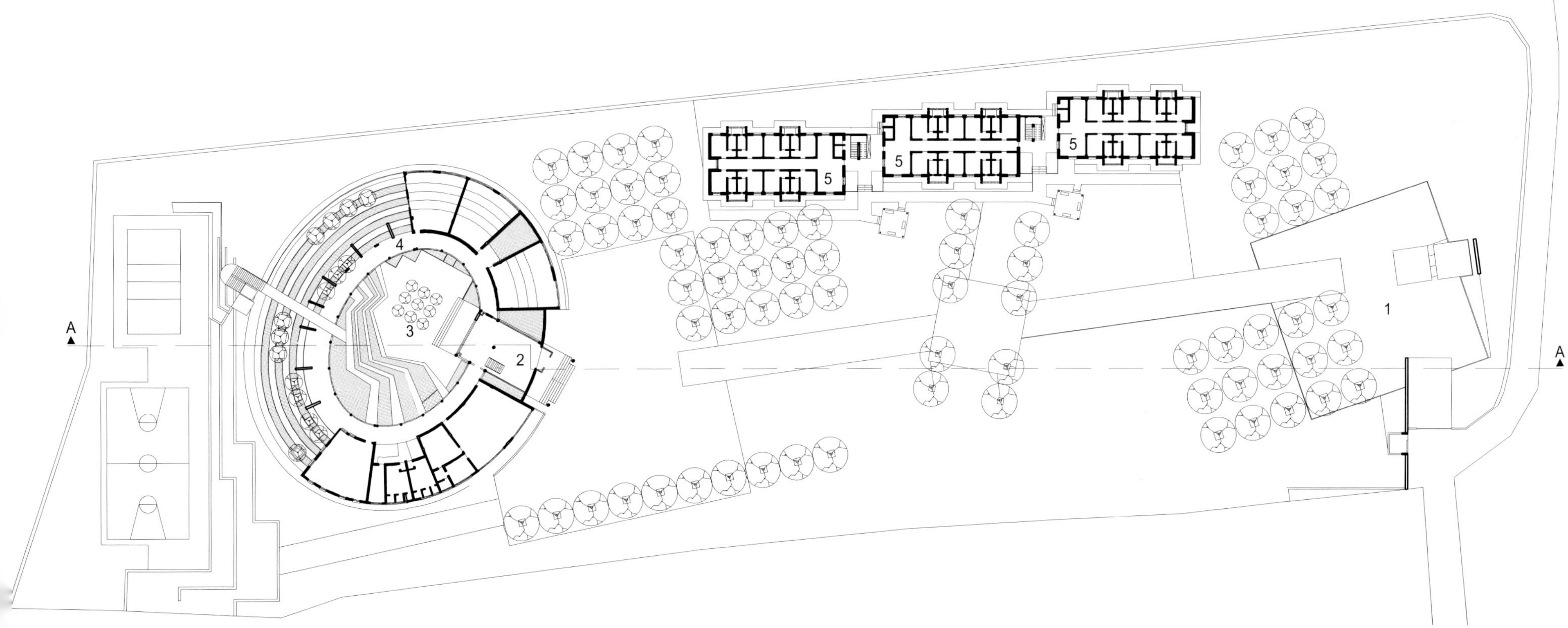

1.ENTRANCE PLAZA
2.ACADEMIC BLOCK
3.AMPHITHEATER
4.FUTURE EXPANSION
5.RESIDENTIAL ACCOMODATION

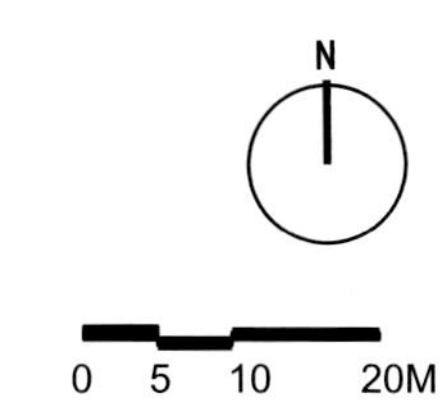

Page 80,81: The residential block reflects the character of MMDC.
Page 82,83: A medley of surface textures enhanced by fenestration.
Left: Pockets of daylight and greenery provide visual relief.

KUSUMAGRAJ MEMORIAL

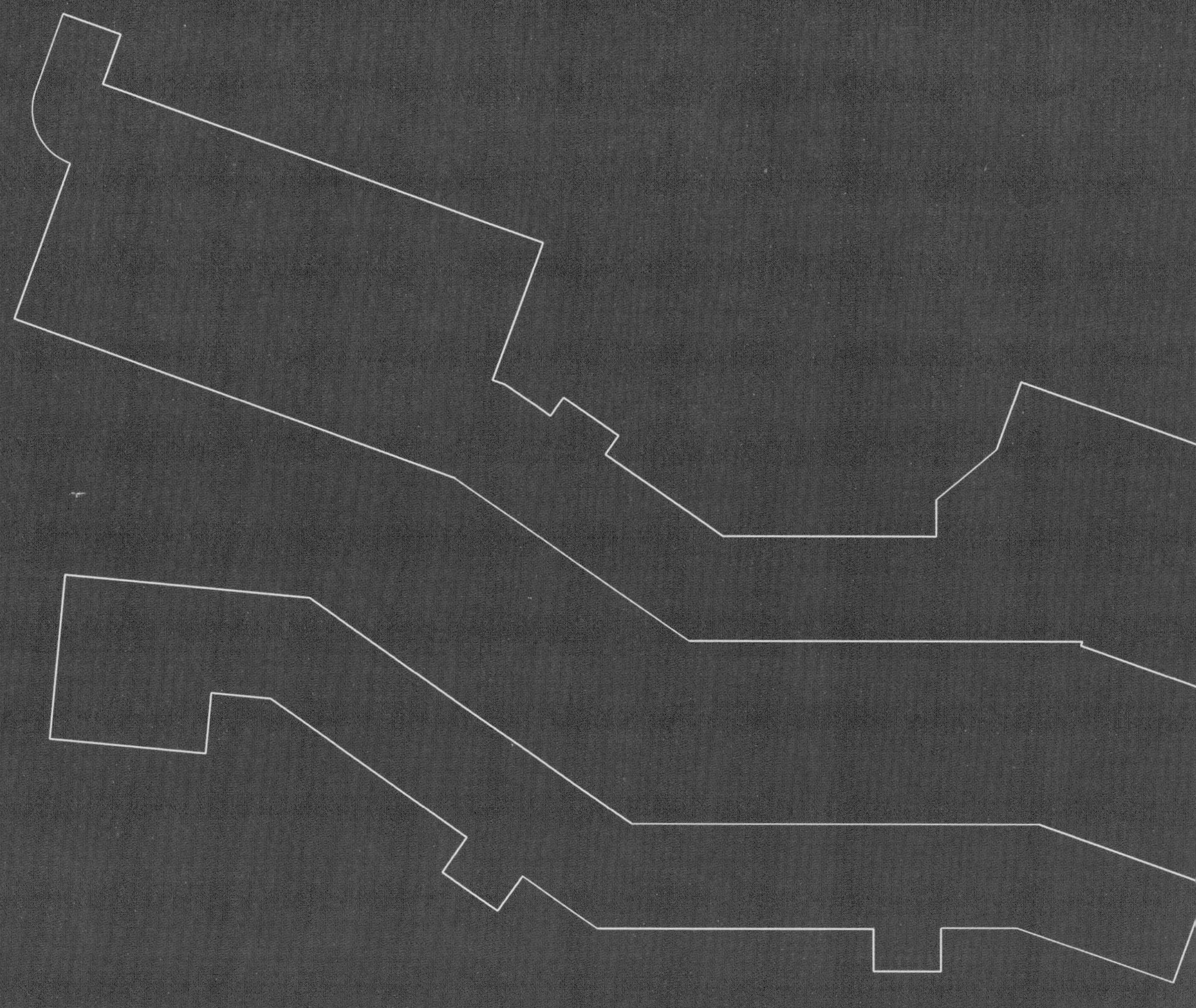

2004

Above: Kadamb trees pay tribute to the writer who revered them.

How does one pay tribute to a personality as legendary as V. V. Shirwadkar? A celebrated Marathi poet and writer known as 'Kusumagraj' to his readers; he was not only a Gyanpith award winner but a humanist, a keen social activist and an eminent literary inspiration to many. Could a piece of architecture do justice to such a personality?

Having envisaged this issue, the members of the Kusumagraj Memorial trust decided to entrust the design to an architect who had been associated with the poet and hence could do justice to his philosophy and character. The selection was thus based was a limited competition amongst three local architects.

The design that came into being is located on a sloping piece of land allotted by the corporation to the trust. Since the land was initially earmarked as a public open space, the architect planned earth-sheltered spaces with the roof used as an accessible garden, hence respecting the original purpose of the land.

The unassuming memorial complex is in sync with the humble, down-to-earth persona of the poet. Swaying 'kadamb' trees dot the entrance, paying a silent tribute to the poet who treasured them the most. The sheltering entrance canopy,

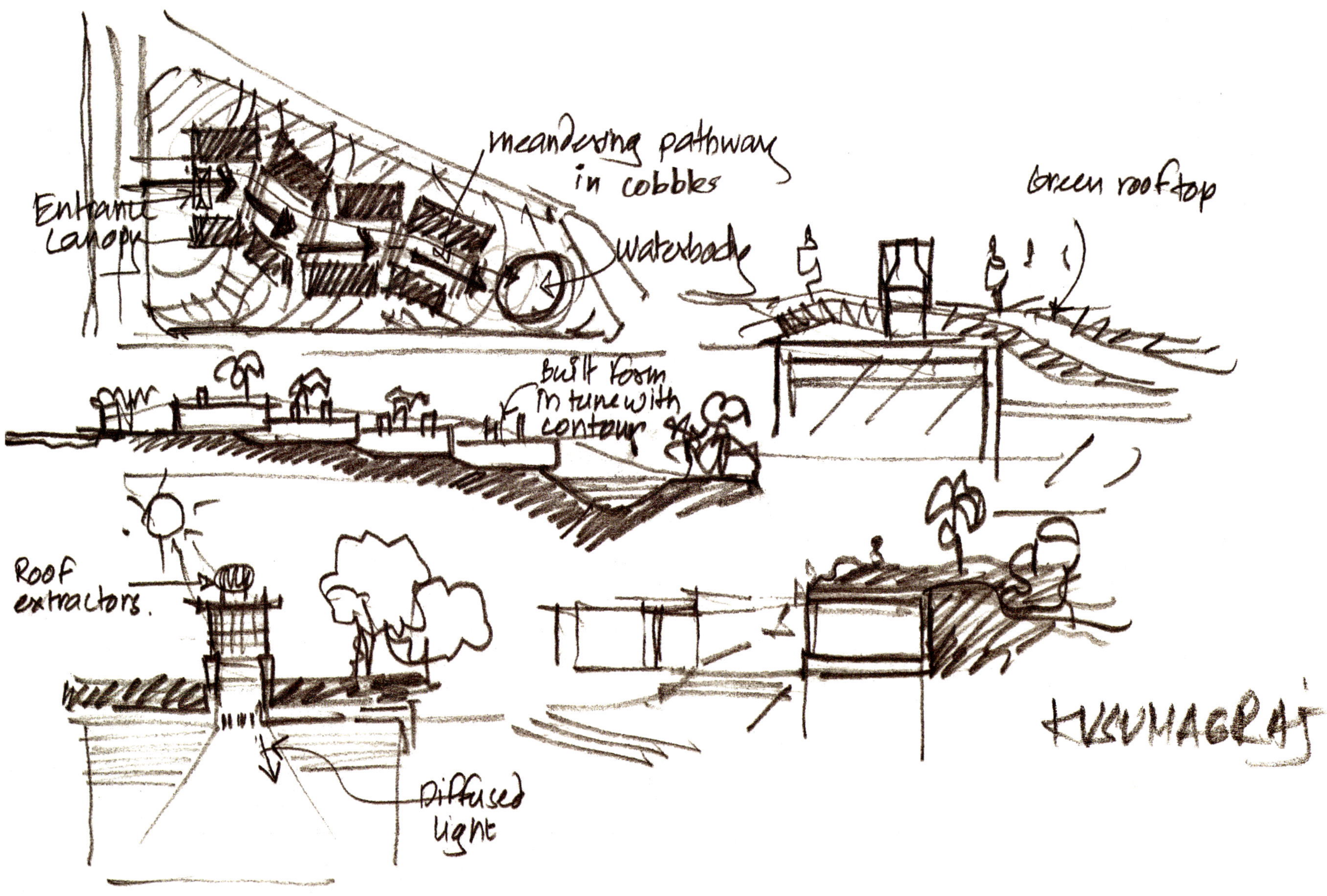
meandering pathway in cobbles
Entrance canopy
waterbody
Green roof top
Built form in tune with contour
Roof extractors.
Diffused light
KUSUMAGRAJ

is another symbolic tribute to the 'Dak bungalows' revered by the writer.

A meandering cobblestoned pathway descends in harmony with the natural site contours, leading the visitor to various activity pockets which include the 'Jeevan Darshan' of the writer, a library, art galleries and seminar rooms. A narrow stream of water clings to its edges providing company to the visitors as they move along. The street finally culminates into the amphitheater serving as an apt focal point.

The canopy and the gradient generated by the steps often serve as a stage, used to conduct debates and discussions on various literary or social issues. The rhythm generated by this circuitous axis creates an interesting series of path and goals and is figurative of how this social activist often chose lesser known roads in his lifetime. The connections formed by concrete bridges tie the roof gardens on both sides. Use of exposed concrete in the spaces and stack ventilation with turbo roof extractors for natural ventilation symbolizes the poet's love for simplicity and truth. Roof gardens soothe the eye with their emerald green spread.

The simple flow of spaces is a strong metaphor of the poet's personality. The entire campus is an echo of the unpretentious life's journey of this greatly revered figure. It is not only a tribute to his past but also a means of keeping his works alive and provides inspiration to the future generations to follow in his footsteps.

A stroll through the Kusumagraj Memorial can prove to be an insightful experience.

Page 90,91: The entrance canopy reminiscent of the 'Dak Bungalows' that the writer loved.
Left: The meandering cobble stoned street flanked by various activity pockets.
Right: The earth-sheltered spaces descend along the street following the natural slope of the site.

कुसुमाग्रज
स्वगत
१९६२ राज्य पुरस्कार 'स्वगत' (काव्यसंग्रह)

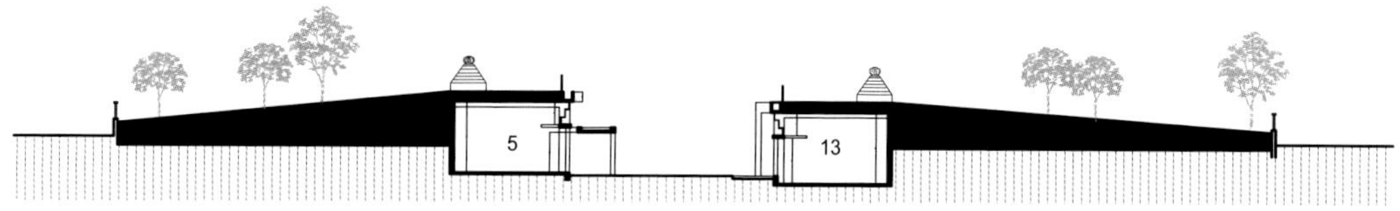

SECTION BB'

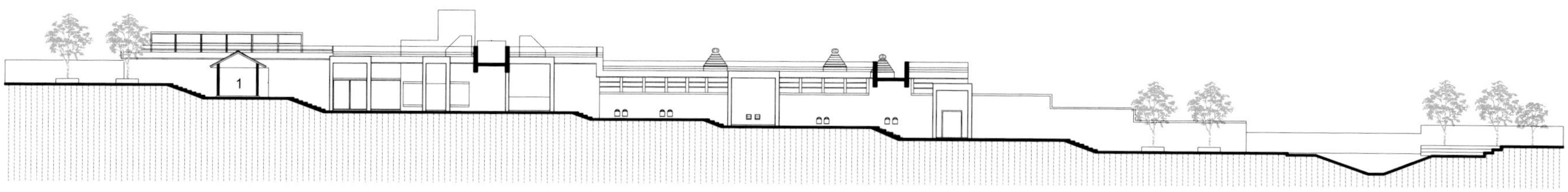

SECTIONAL ELEVATION AA'

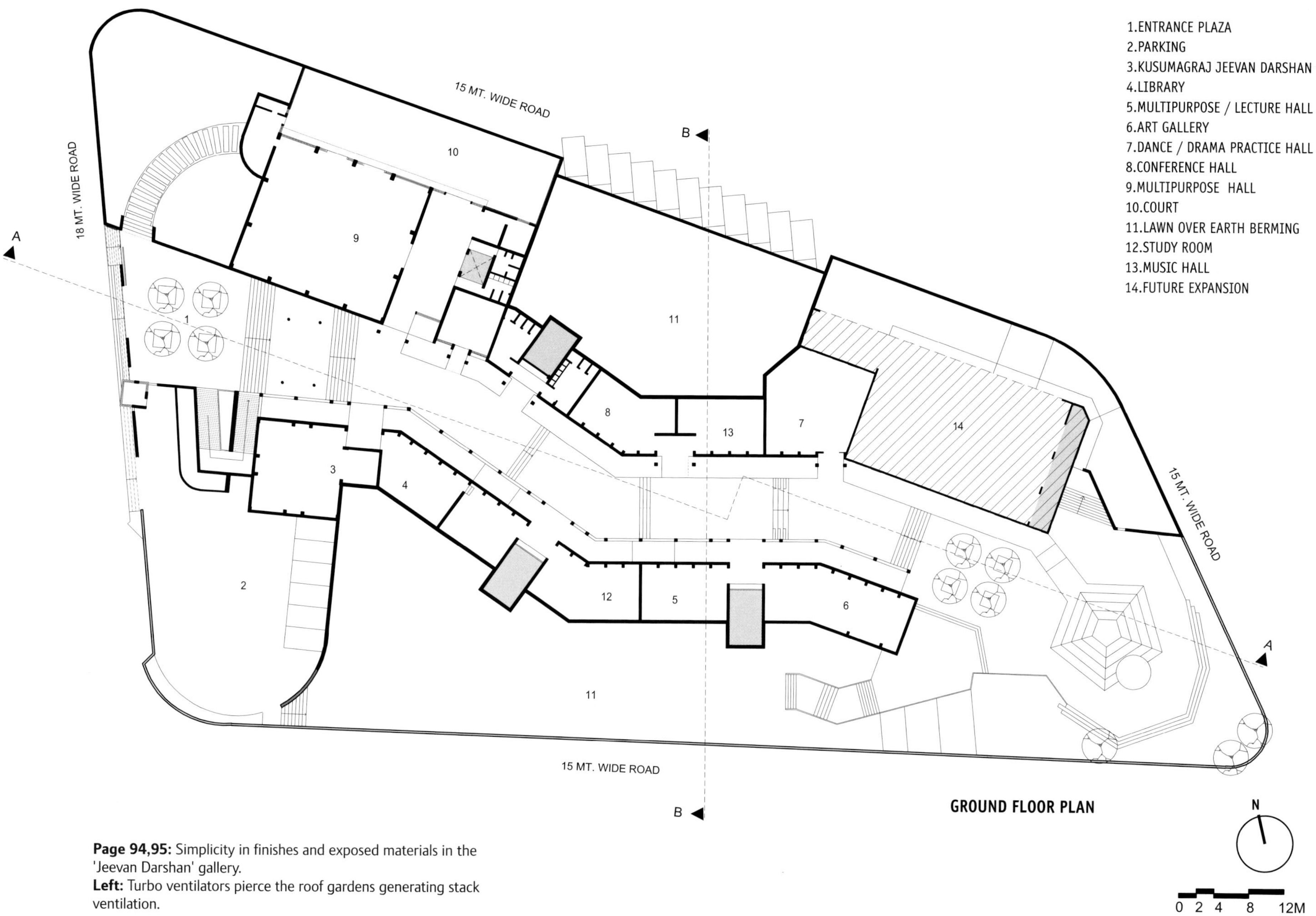

GROUND FLOOR PLAN

Page 94,95: Simplicity in finishes and exposed materials in the 'Jeevan Darshan' gallery.
Left: Turbo ventilators pierce the roof gardens generating stack ventilation.

FARMHOUSE AT MAHIRAVANI

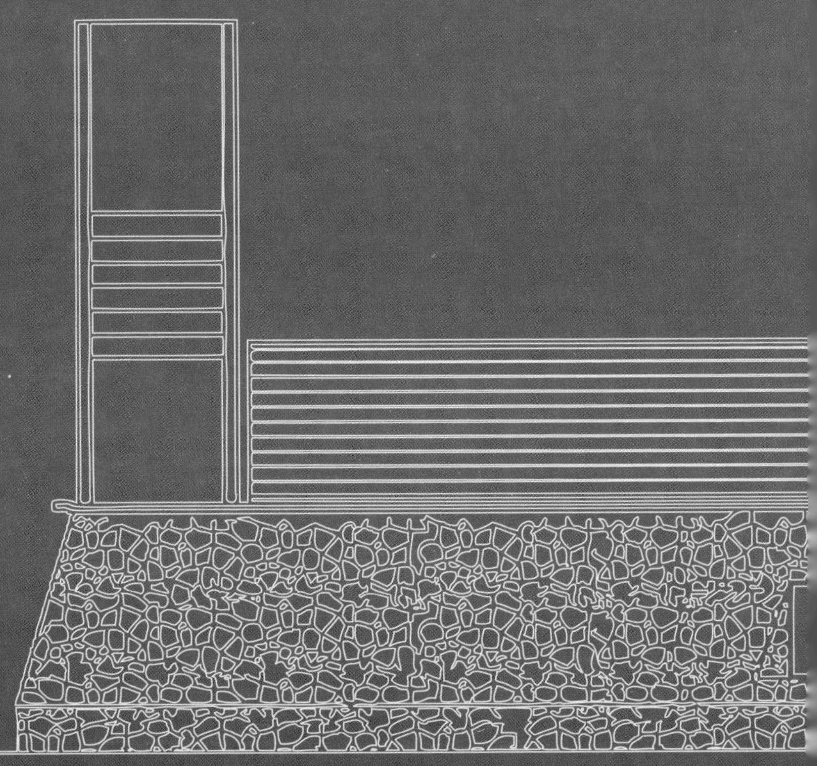

2005

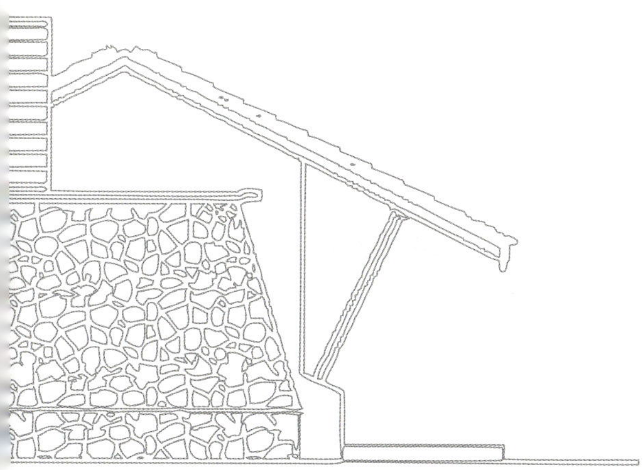

Above: A glimpse of the swimming pool

Off the main city roads of Nashik, an inconspicuous little path branches off unexpectedly towards a dam and a dense clump of trees beyond. There is nothing to indicate to an average passerby what lies beyond this otherwise modest countryside.

However, to those who know their way, this path only serves as a build up to the little hideout that lies beyond; a personal space for the architect and his family. For the first time visitor who trudges over the dam and makes way through the wooded surrounds, it is ambiguity at its best. Finally, the sloping stone walls of the farmhouse emerge from the earth, beckoning the visitor inside.

The sounds of chirping birds and humming bees, the slope of the sheltering roof and a touch of the cool terracotta floor under one's feet create the perfect entrance transition and draw you into the courtyard at the heart of the space. The lotus court draws you in further with its tranquil aura. The champa court and the bamboo court on either side craft a tapestry of light and shade. The utter simplicity of the plan doubles the impact.

The distinction generated by the roughness of the stones with the warmth of terracotta and wood, the sharp edges of gravel softened by the

tenderness of natural leaves and the calmness of water; all add up to a innate sense of positivity and harmony. A placid swimming pool rests outside, merging beautifully with the surroundings.

The story of how the space actually evolved is set around a series of arches retrieved from an old wada and preserved by the architect for over two decades. The spaces thus evolved are framed by these arches and are notable for the absence of formal walls, doors and windows, allowing for a seamless visual and physical connect between the covered and uncovered spaces.

Built on the principles of sustainable architecture and minimalist living, the design is a reflection of local architecture and conducive to the composite climate of the region. A water harvesting pond connected to percolation pits and trenches in the bare ground helps recycle water on site. Solar panels are used for water heating and part of other electrical consumption adding to the sustainability in the design.

The stone used in the masonry work has been quarried from a well dug on the site itself.
The otherwise arid and barren piece of land was transformed by planting a mixed culture of around 4000 medicinal, flowering and fruit bearing trees; thus creating a microcosm conducive to providing a home to birds and other organisms in the neighborhood.

This farmhouse is symbolic of all the things the architect loves and respects. The elements of nature – a piece of sky, touch of the earth, access to wind and the presence of water are all nurtured here. Functionally it is a multi-utility space, serving as a weekend home to unwind and entertain as well as a weekend studio to discuss art, architecture and life. The space is designed to welcome all seasons and the bounties they bring.

Above all, it is a melting pot for different ideologies on art, architecture and life.

Is this a space to meditate or a workshop to discuss ideas? Or are these two eventually the same? And more importantly, is it really a built space or just nature rearranged? - you wonder. This farmhouse leaves you with many questions to ponder about and yet a day spent here can provide answers to many of life's questions.

Left: Rustic stone walls frame the main entrance.

Left: Deep roof overhangs and the organic landscape beyond.
Right: Stone quarried from the site used for constructing walls and planter beds.

Left: Inward looking spaces converge into the central courtyard.
Right: Terracotta floors team up with the water element to build contrasts with the stone.

Above: Discuss, eat and savour the surrounds in this unusual dining space.

Above: A seating by the poolside with a connecting bridge.

Left: The lotus court sheltered by a pergola.
Above: Variety of floor textures stimulate the senses

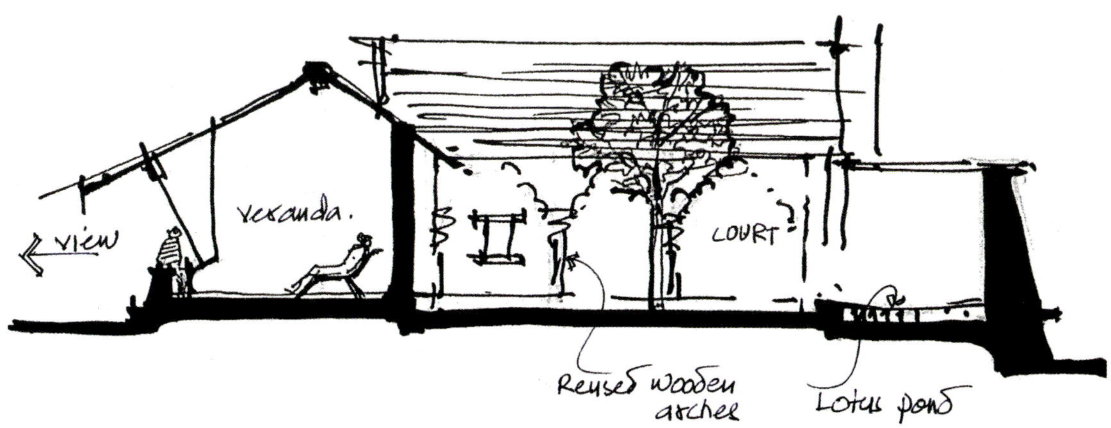

Left: A multipurpose space to interact, perform or unwind.

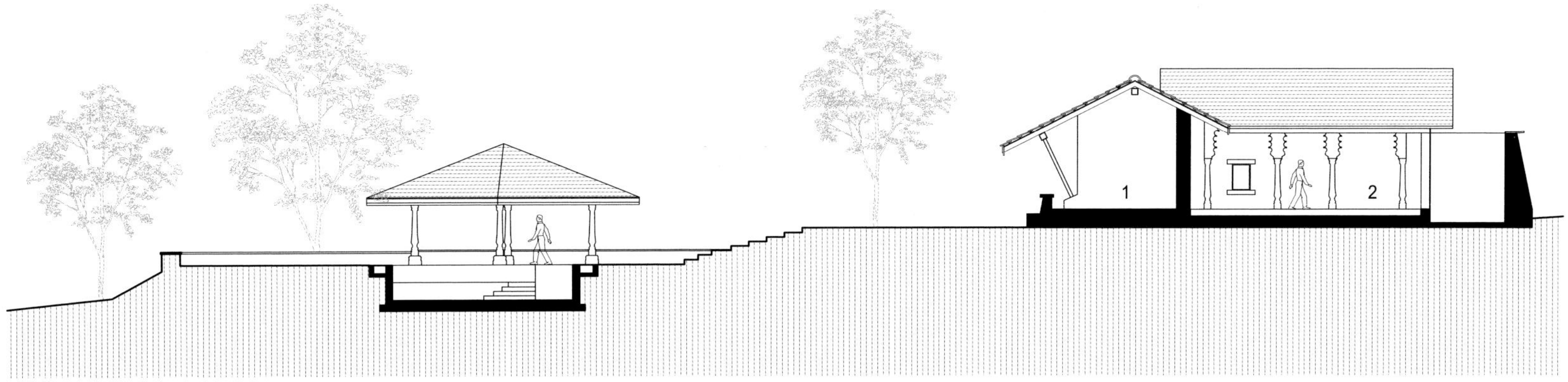

SECTION AA

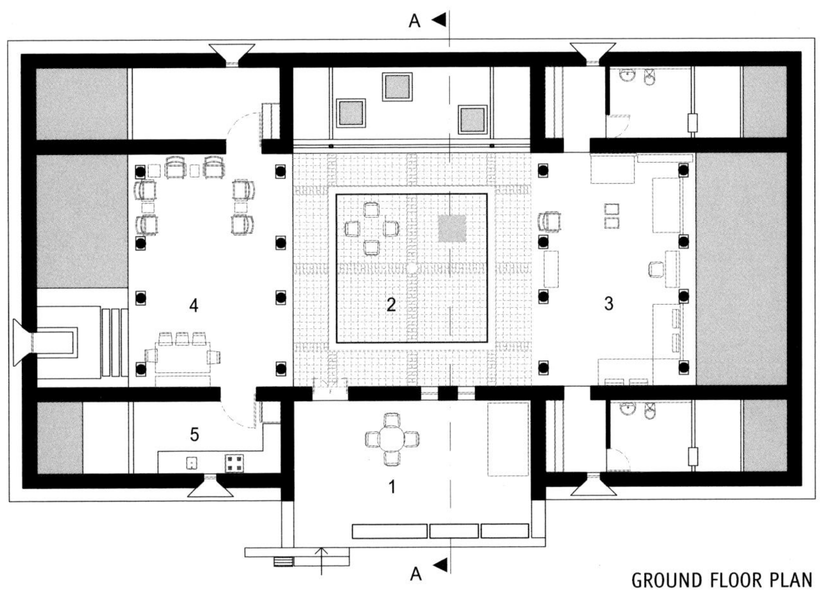

GROUND FLOOR PLAN

1.VERANDAH
2.COURTYARD
3.MULTIPLE USE SPACE
4.DINING / LIVING
5.KITCHEN

N

0 1 3 7M

1.ENTRANCE TO SITE
2.FARMHOUSE
3.SWIMMING POOL
4.SERVANT QUARTERS
5.HARVESTING POND
6.WELL
7.FILTRATION PLANT ROOM
8.VERMICULTURE PITS
9.LAWN
10.LAWN MOUND
11.BAMBOO GROVE

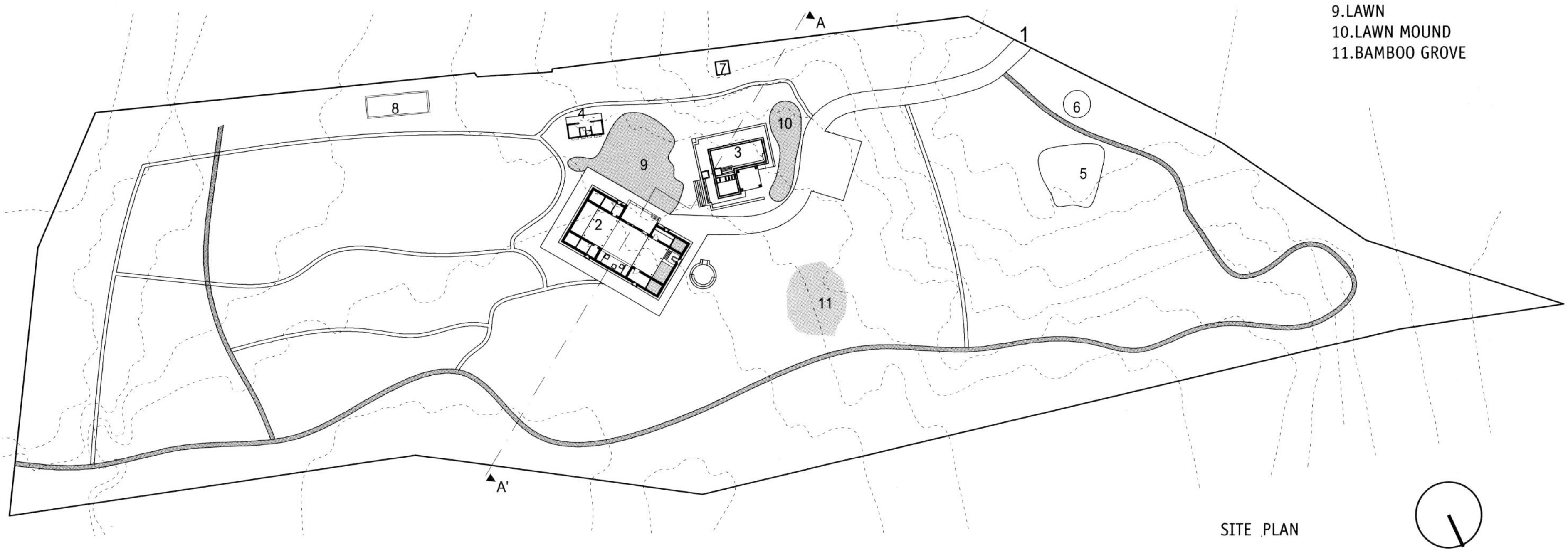

SITE PLAN

N

0 5 10 20M

Left: Wooden arches retrieved from an old wada and preserved by the architect for two decades.

BAPAT BAGWE RESIDENCE

2007

'Space Therapy' is a word that comes to mind, when one experiences this weekend retreat. Located on a large expanse of agricultural land in the outskirts of Nashik, this farmhouse has all the natural elements of earth, water and air, needed to relax and rejuvenate one's body and soul.

The farmhouse caters to two families who needed a space that was connected but still unhindered in terms of privacy. The purpose of the space is largely to provide a break from the monotony of a busy routine in life. The success of the design lay in luring the user back into its fold again and again to experience the calming effect it provides.

The initial thought process started with the idea of raising the site to get a clear view of the dam it faced. Thus, earth excavated from a nearby harvesting pond has been reused to elevate the entire strip on which the built form has been placed.

A meandering pathway leads to two entrances transiting into separate spaces to serve the two families. Curved walls in coursed stone masonry flow into each other defining the separate units and yet creating a deep interlocking of spaces. Semi hidden gardens lead to living areas beyond and form a harmonious composition of free flowing planes and orthogonal built forms. At this

Above: The discreet main entrance.

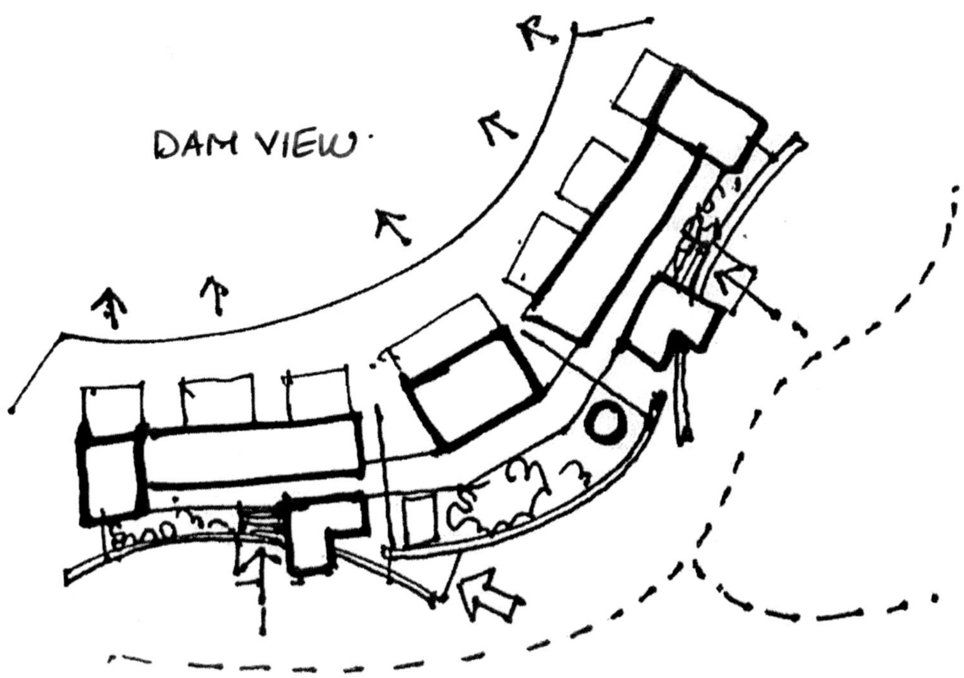

Left top: Coursed stone masonry walls screen the private spaces.
Left bottom: Sweeping curves accentuated by horizontal stone bands.

point the dam which was hidden from view so far is revealed.

The covered sit-outs emerging out of every room spill over into the surrounding sloping lawns and create an echo towards the water body beyond. As the sun paints the sky in vibrant colours every evening, these levels form the perfect setting to enjoy nature's flawless performance.

Modern and traditional materials form a harmonious confluence in this farmhouse, making divergence one of the striking elements in the design approach. Structural steel, glass and cement fibre board roofing go hand in hand with natural materials like stone, cane and wood. Fine detailing in the composition of steps at the entrance and the free edging to the sit outs add emphasis to form.

This farmhouse can be best described as a rhythmic composition strung together along the thread of green spaces; its comfort and tranquillity compelling the user to come back into its fold on every possible pretext.

Left: Daylight throwing patterns on the inner surfaces
Right: Daylight filters into the courtyard and the connecting passage

Page 120,121: Living areas surrounded by patches of green.
Page 122,123: All activities spilling out towards the dam.
Above: View of the unified cluster converging towards the dam side.

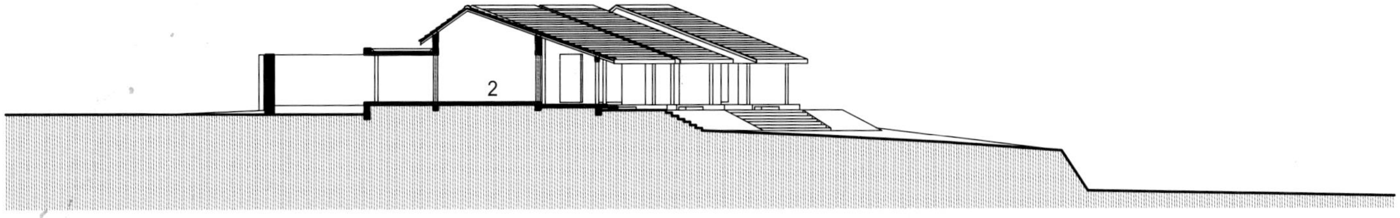

SECTION AA

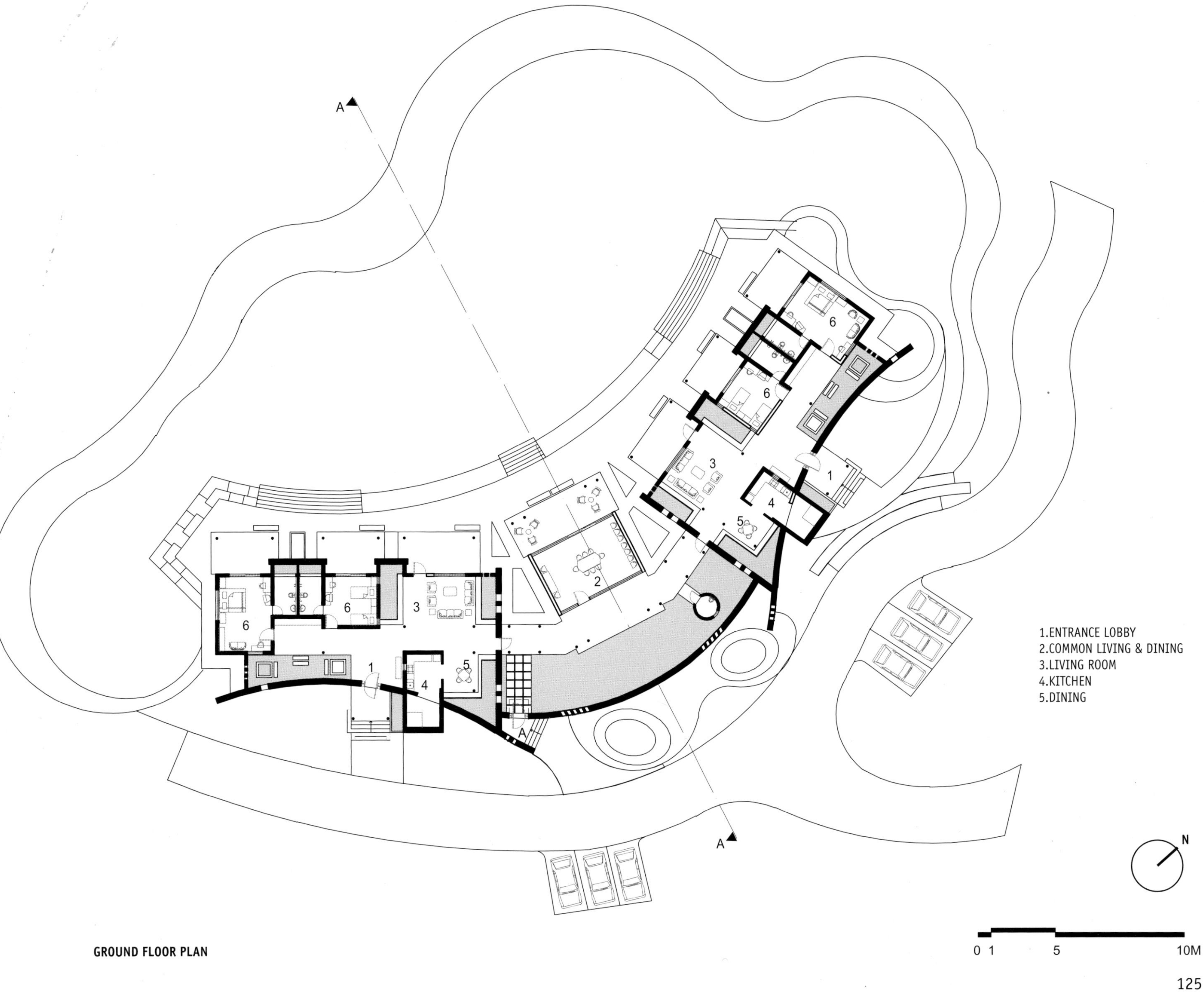

GROUND FLOOR PLAN

RASANE RESIDENCE

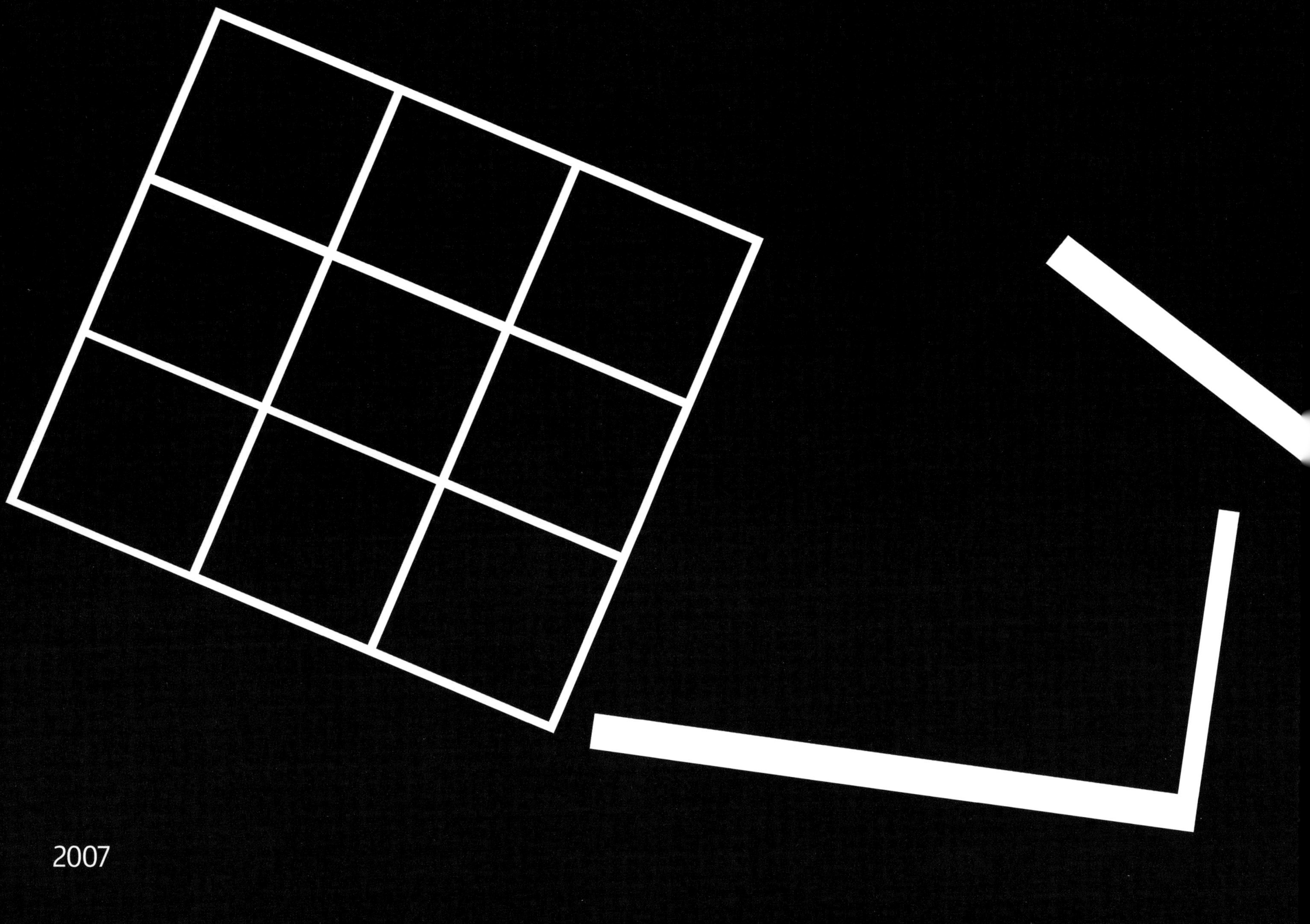

2007

A bungalow around the corner of the street is a very common occurrence in the residential neighborhoods of Nashik. But when you come across one which stands out for its striking contrasts, one is tempted to explore further. This residence is one such expression which uses the basic design elements of points, lines and planes in a rhythmic way to create a visually striking composition.

The main entrance is an interesting journey. Tilted horizontal planes form bridges and steps over a water pool creating an axis leading to the main structure. A series of inclined walls, clad in organized patterns of local stone define the entrance lobby making it wide and welcoming. The otherwise orthogonal grid of the structure is cleverly broken by these planes.

The living spaces at the ground floor are interspersed by open to sky pockets, lush with soft landscape flowing into the spaces effortlessly. Pools of daylight dot the living, dining, stairway and pooja room, binding them together as one entity. The patterned stone walls wrap around inside the building creating a continuity in the character. The private spaces at the upper floor connect to these areas below through the

Above: A composition of lines and planes.

Left: Patterns of lines give a sense of direction.

Right: Landscape elements breaking the orthogonal grid.

Left: The composition of planes as viewed from the street.

numerous voids and experience the tranquillity of nature.

Water has been used as an element throughout the design in various forms ranging from still water pools at the entrance to water cascades within the house. Contrast is well explored by using rough coursed stone against smooth white wall surfaces. Flooring in silky Italian marble goes hand in hand with textured stone pavers and earthy pebbles. Accents of vibrant colours stand out against a white background. A steel and glass canopy covers the entrance porch, its transparency complementing the opaque stone behind. Built and unbuilt, light and shade, rough and smooth all add up to a distinct play of contrasts.

Patterns using lines build yet another strong expression of design. The garden wall, gate and the entrance transition is a composition of lines interpreted in textured stone, wooden slats and garden seats. Small square openings in the walls and roof, cubes and lights dotting the entrance, balcony projections emerging from the facade all represent a point as an element at varying scales.This bold approach to materials and design elements develops a new vocabulary and transforms a minimalist design into an eye-catching outcome.

Below: Soft landscape and diffused daylight flowing through the living and dining areas.

Left: The courtyard serves as a visual link between floors.

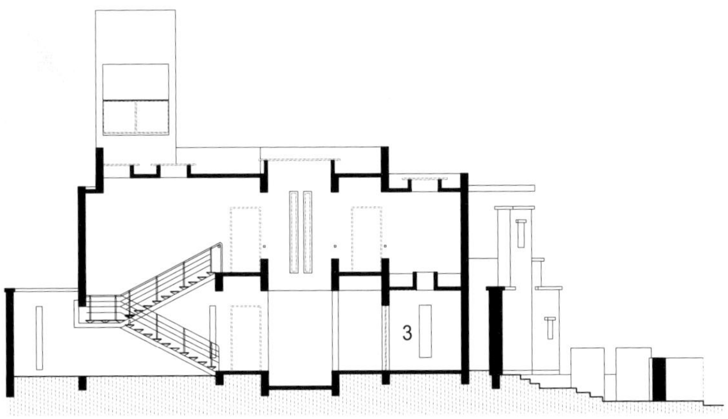

SECTION AT AA

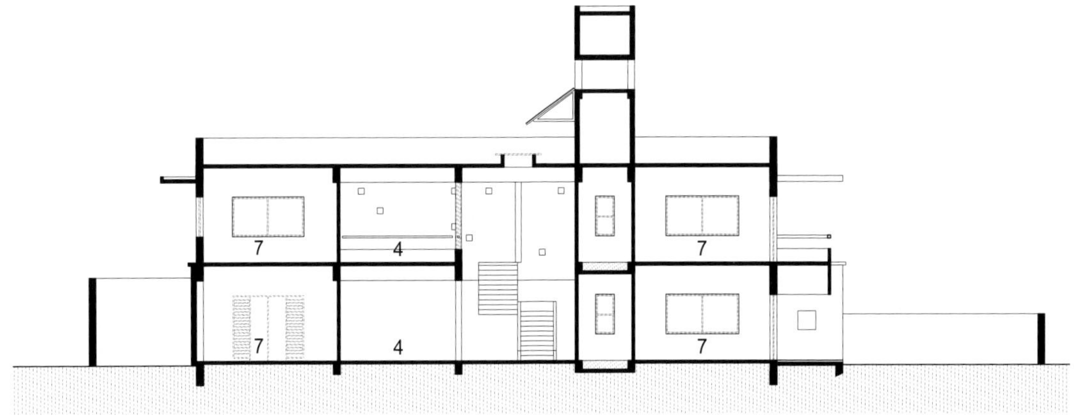

SECTION AT BB

1.ENTRANCE LOBBY
2.LIVING ROOM
3.POOJA ROOM
4.FAMILY SEATING
5.DINING
6.KITCHEN
7.BEDROOM
8.COVERED TERRACE
9.COVERED PARKING
10.VEGETABLE GARDEN

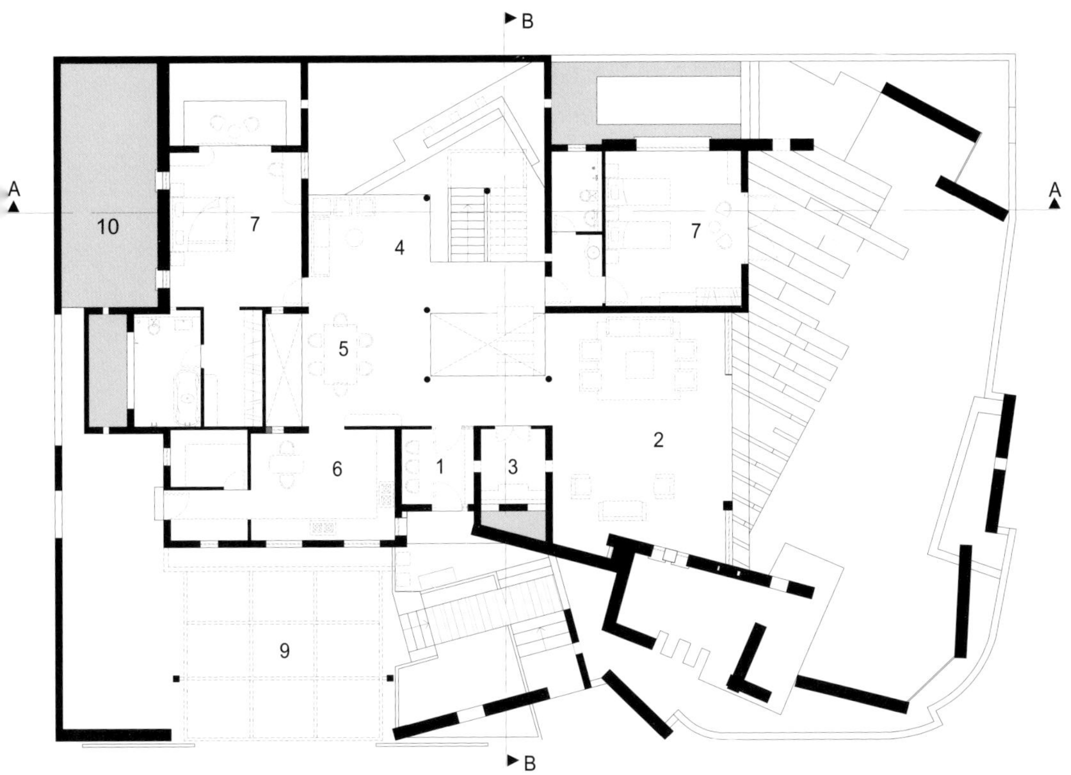

GROUND FLOOR PLAN

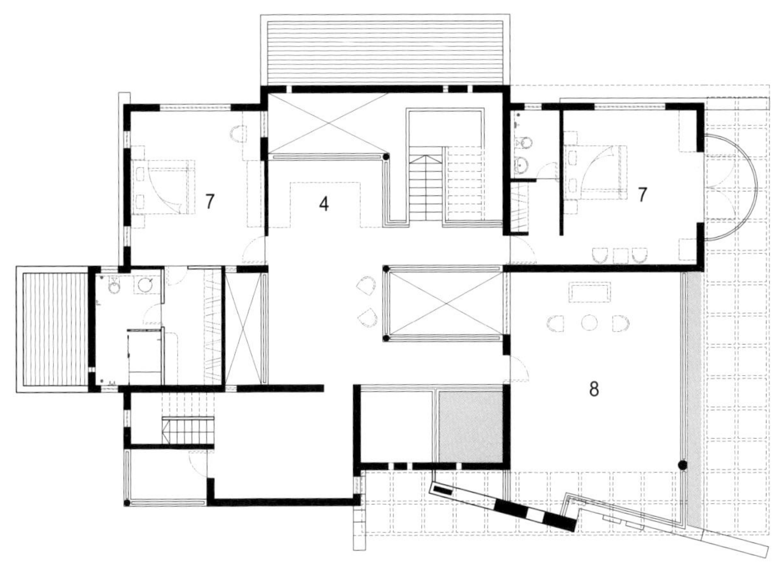

FIRST FLOOR PLAN

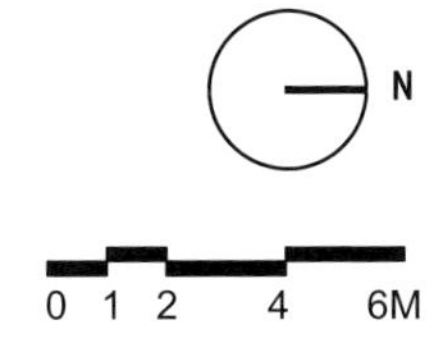

RAOSAHEB PATIL RESIDENCE

2007

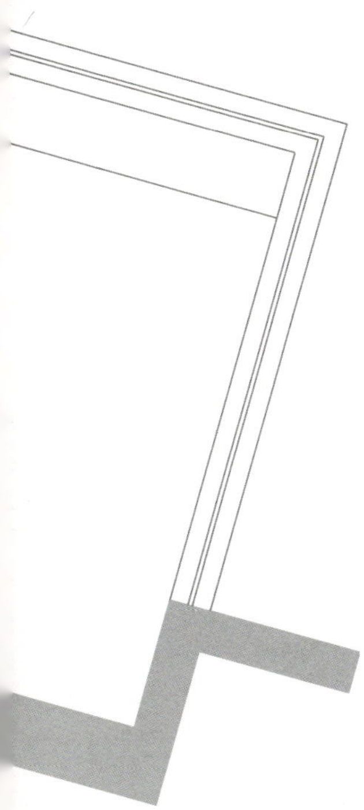

Above: The sheltering entrance porch.

This house is a perfect study in how ambiguity as a design expression can be used to create maximum impact. The entry to the house is deliberately underplayed. A nondescript gate leads to a ramp climbing upwards to the main entrance. The ascent of the ramp gives no clue as to what lies ahead. The scene reaches a crescendo when you reach the top and the breathtaking view of the river Godavari engulfs you.

A placid lily pond and a half hidden garden beyond arouse one's curiosity. The entrance lobby is well protected with a double height roof. A cantilever balcony overlooking the entrance lobby creates a vertical link and an interesting addition of form to the space.

Rustic walls serve as a contrast to the frames in painted white. Slender double height circular columns hold up the sheltering slopes of the roofs.

As one steps into the living spaces beyond, a composition of salvaged wood and yellow jaisalmer flooring, rattan furniture, and tiny accents of colour add the desired texture and warmth. Corner windows throughout the rooms create a language of their own and drench the spaces in daylight. The raised garden beyond the windows forges a connection to the earth even at

Page 138,139: A view from the abutting street capturing the composition of volumes.
Page140,141: A glimpse of the river from the corner window.
Left: The open stairway flows into to the dining space.
Right: Indoors and outdoors meet in the covered veranda

this height. Window seats form compact hobby spaces to unwind. The house narrates stories of old adventures and travel through bric-a-brac from the client's collection that blend in seamlessly with the space.

The view framed by the uninterrupted glazing to the north captures different angles of the Godavari, the lush green shrubbery around it and the endless void of the sky beyond. The serenity of this view is echoed in the two staggered courtyards in the house, each lush with foliage reaching up to the spaces above.

A glass and wood elevator emerges from within the courtyard, reaching into the sunbathed study at the upper level.

The private spaces at the upper level include the daughter's room which serves as a canvas for her bright floral art work. The outdoor deck outside the master bedroom reaches out to the garden outside and the river beyond. The lowermost level houses a gym and a swimming pool. The space derives daylight from skylit pockets on the periphery and also uses natural materials such as bamboo, natural rough stone and wood.

The client's sensitivity to sustainable design has led to the use of features like cavity walls and salvaged wood from their personal collection to build the furniture and flooring. Water bodies and convective cooling through the courtyard ensure thermal comfort. Exposed rain water pipes channelize rain water and harvest it. The design is intrinsically climate responsive and energy efficient. The design reflects a very strong connection to its surroundings, a harmony with natural elements and resonates with the serenity of the facing river.

Left: A ramp leads to the main entrance.

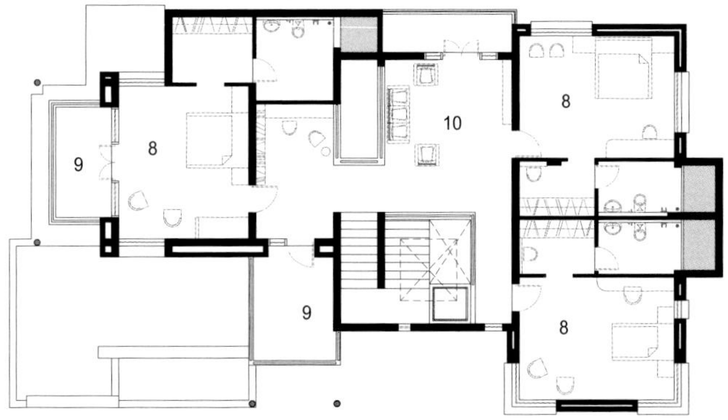

FIRST FLOOR PLAN

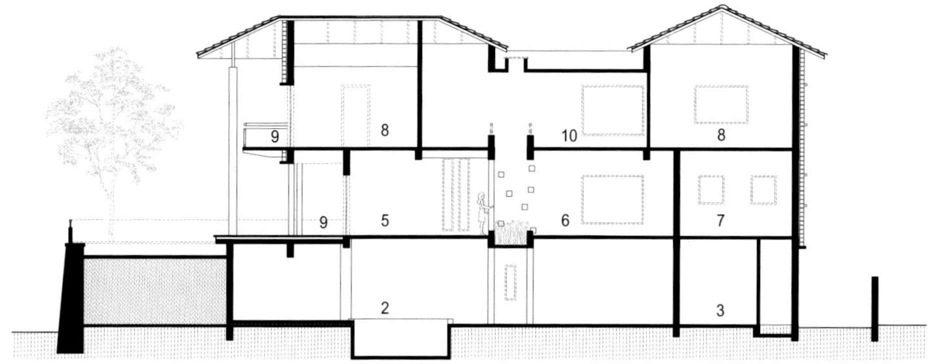

SECTION AA

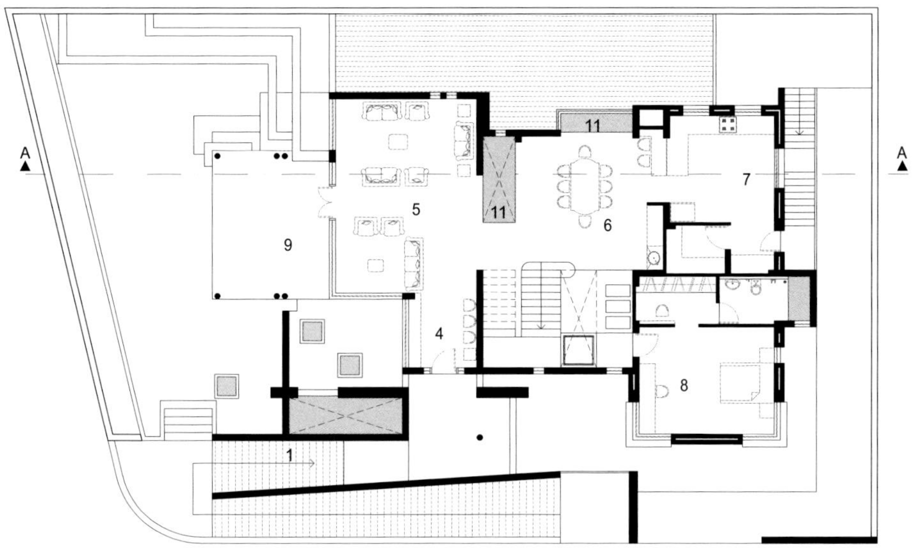

STILT FLOOR PLAN

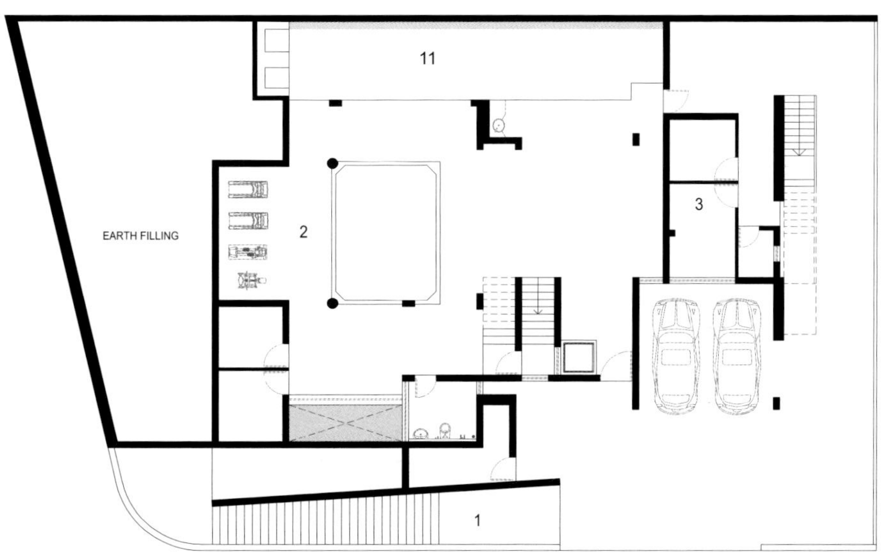

GROUND FLOOR PLAN

1. ENTRANCE RAMP
2. EXERCISE POOL / GYMNASIUM
3. SERVANT QUARTERS
4. ENTRANCE LOBBY
5. LIVING ROOM
6. DINING
7. KITCHEN
8. BEDROOM
9. SIT OUT
10. FAMILY SEATING
11. COURT

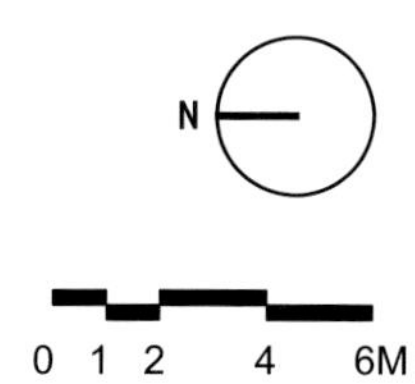

2007

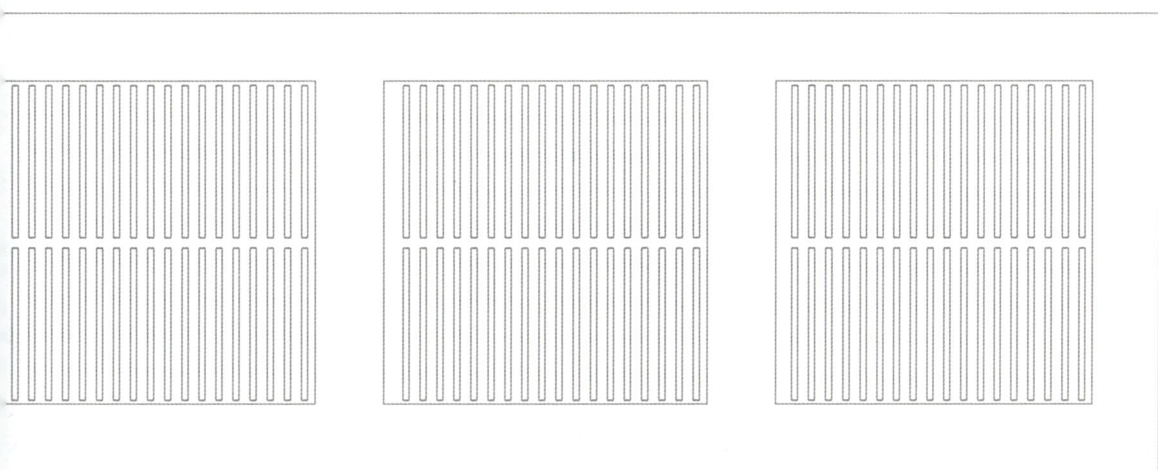

Above: Vertical louvers in square modules define a vocabulary of design.

The design of an institutional building campus can have a profound impact on the young minds of the students who use the facility. The campus of Bhujbal Knowledge City is one such example of excellence in structural engineering and the ability to develop a novel design approach in order to offset the project time constraints. Situated on a thirty three acre parcel of land, the Bhujbal Knowledge City is a stimulating environment for innovative ideas to be nurtured.

Built on a fast track schedule, the campus reveals a vocabulary of design that uses modular planning, scale and height variation to interpret the needs of the design brief. A massive organic curve forms the roof of the entrance to the campus, a suitable metaphor to the vision of the institute and its goals. A thoughtfully designed structural system holds up massive spans, generating rhythm and dynamism. An example of innovation in engineering, it is meant to serve as an inspiration to the budding engineers in the campus. A curved north facing glazed wall bathes the lobby and the library beyond with diffused daylight.

Beyond this, the campus is composed of orthogonal modules spread in a simple grid across the triangular site. The various departments are located in these pods each with a central focal

MET

point in the form of a courtyard. These modules are then bound together by an elevated circular walkway providing a contrast to the otherwise strictly orthogonal design vocabulary. This circle embraces a generously landscaped interaction space. The accentuated column connections along the circular pathway enhance the form and the structure of the bridge.

Each module is defined by a simple grid of square openings. Shading devices envelop the periphery and a subtraction of volume carves out the entrance lobby. Daylight seeps in through internal courtyards which are all treated differently, again using simple geometric forms and sculptural plant species. Accents of vibrant colour stimulate the senses.

The design vocabulary of geometric forms finds coherence in the geometric patterns of landscape, fenestration and flooring patterns, generating an echo in the entire campus. The amphitheater that the users naturally gravitate towards, echo the stepped character of the ghats of the Godavari in old Nashik.

Time constraint can prove to be a tough challenge for any project. Bhujbal Knowledge City campus therefore is a remarkable study in how an adaptable approach can convert the project constraints into highlights of the design.

However, this approach has not altered the fundamental philosophy of the architect which involves profuse use of nature, sustainable design and user comfort. Smart detailing, modular design approach and innovative use of material come together to bring about spaces that are functional, dynamic and lively.

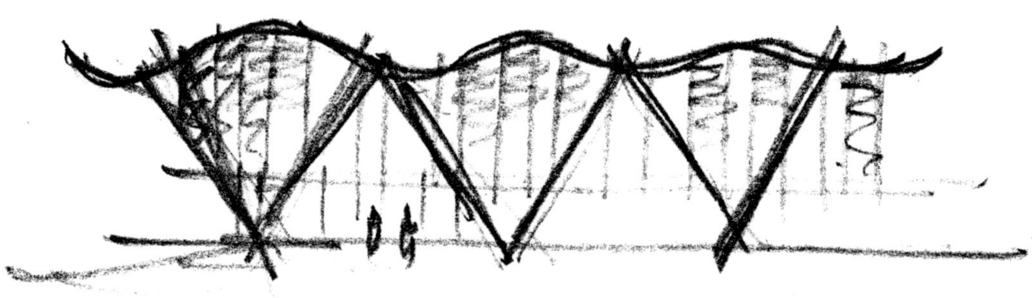

Left: Pathways branching of from the main entrance.

Page 150: The elevated circular walkway connecting the modules.
Page 151: The accentuated column connections enhance the structure of the bridge.
Left : The cafeteria block extending into the outdoor spaces
Right: The vocabulary of simple frames find an echo in the campus.

MET
Bhujbal
Knowledge City
PHARMACY
MANAGEMENT
ENGINEERING
DISTANCE LEARNING
I.T.
POLYTECHNIC

Left top: A glimpse of the sculptural entrance canopy.
Left bottom: Fringes of green around the built spaces.
Right: Minimalist landscape in varying grid patterns.

Page 156,157: The dynamic main entrance canopy sheltering the glazing behind.
Left: Endemic plant species dot the campus.
Right: Internal landscaped atrium within a learning module.

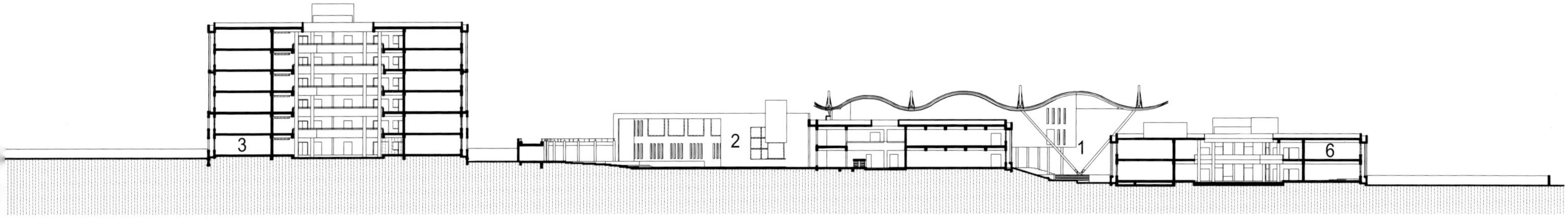

SECTION AA

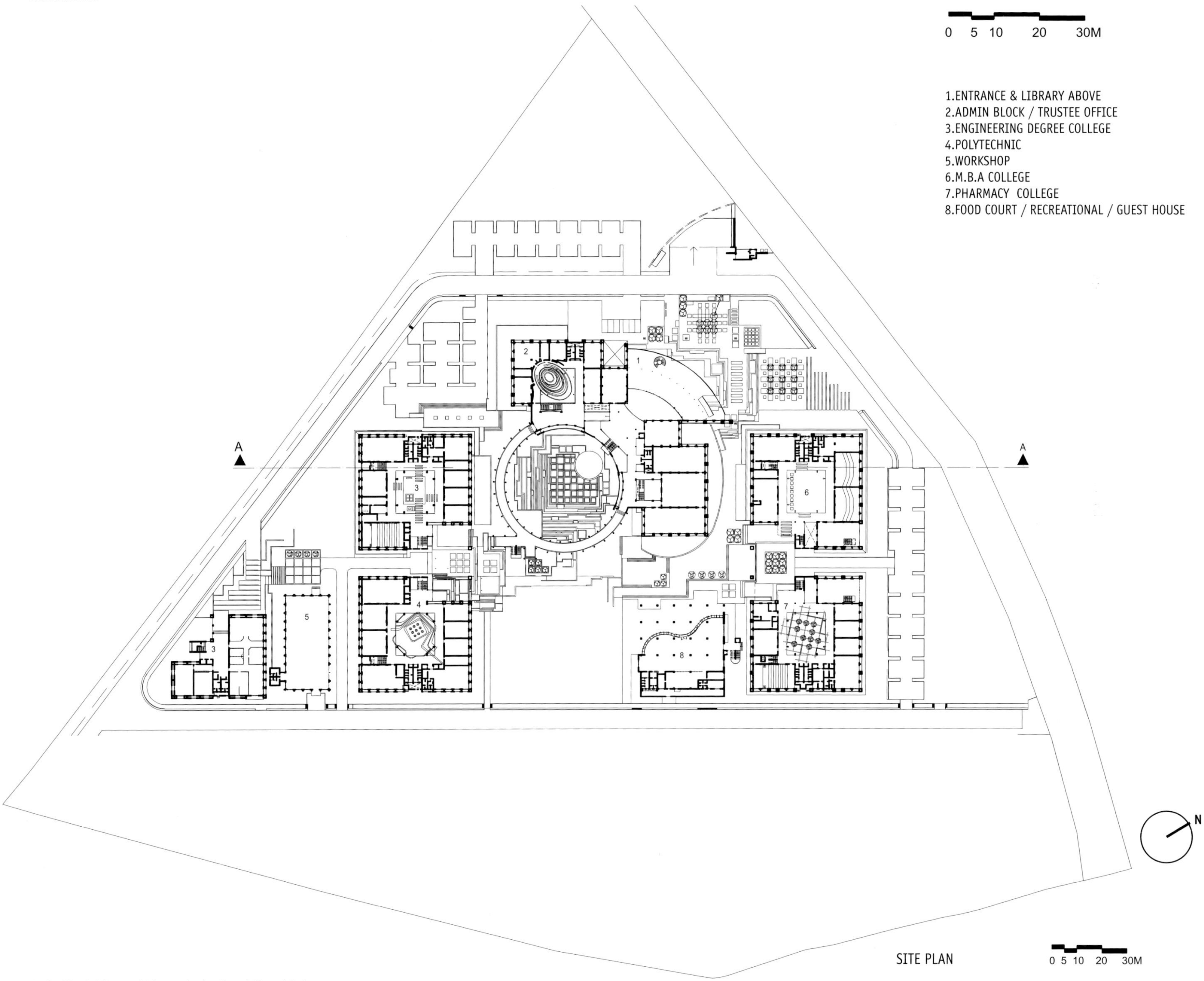

SITE PLAN

Left: The lobby and library bathed in diffused light

GOLIYA RESIDENCE

2008

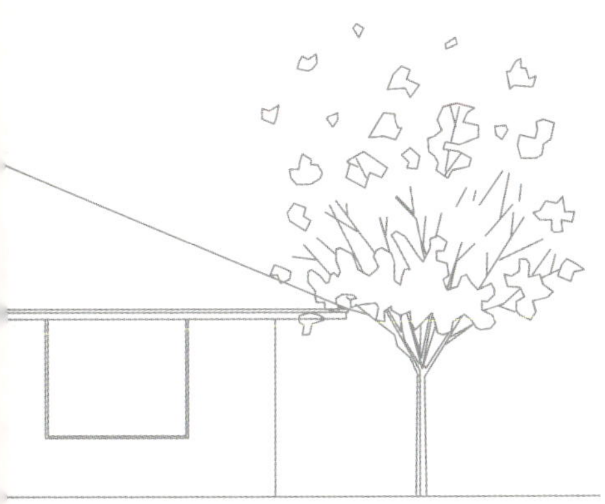

Above: The sunken kund forming a seating space.

This design is a reflection of the deep bonding between the architect and the client over two decades and having designed a number of spaces for them.

The concept has evolved from a clear mandate from the client of needing all activities at one level to foster interaction within the family members.

Located on a group of plots on the outskirts of the city, vastushastra guidelines directed that the structure be placed at the south-west corner of the plot and the entrance to the north-east. A covered bridge flanked by water and landscape on either side, spans this distance making the approach to the house a refreshing journey. The bridge provides the major axis in the design, forging a connection with the main structure that lies beyond.

The entrance lobby at the end of the bridge draws you into the quiet reverie of the house. The sprawling living space is interspersed with three skylit spaces creating a dramatic tapestry of light and shade. The echo and unity of spaces is enhanced by the use of increased height and warm colours.

The central courtyard leads you visually towards a Buddha figurine at the end of the space forming a

Left: The covered bridge leading to the main structure.
Right: Exposed concrete slab with organic patterns.

Left: The sprawling living area interspersed with three skylit spaces.

strong centrepiece of the design. The courtyard to the right is made integral to the living space by creating a sunken sitting circle within, reminiscent of an ancient kund. As one turns to the left, a beautiful composition of steps forms a natural place to sit and relax.

The private areas are all laid out around the central space with connecting louvered windows making the house entirely inward looking. The family room however overlooks the lush landscaped stretch of green, visually and functionally balancing the series of voids within the house.

The design approach in this case was a response to the clients' North Indian roots. The generosity of movement and levels of scale that this space provides is evocative of the ancient havelis of India. As a paradox, the space layout, use of materials and detailing are modern and cater to today's lifestyle.

Opulence is an expression which is not easy to handle. This design however, displays a mature and balanced approach in this regard. It is an expression of a contemporary design vocabulary infused with the nostalgia of tradition.

Left: Vertical connections and a skylit stairway.
Right: Sloping roof in wood and steel.

Below: A distant view captures the entire site.

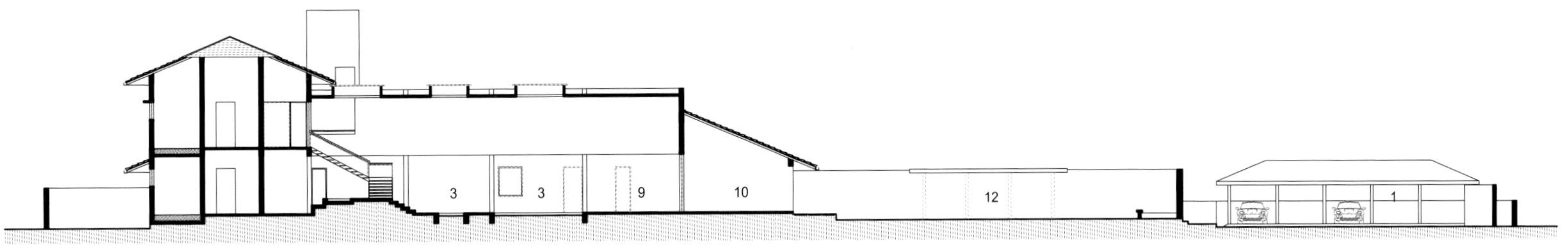

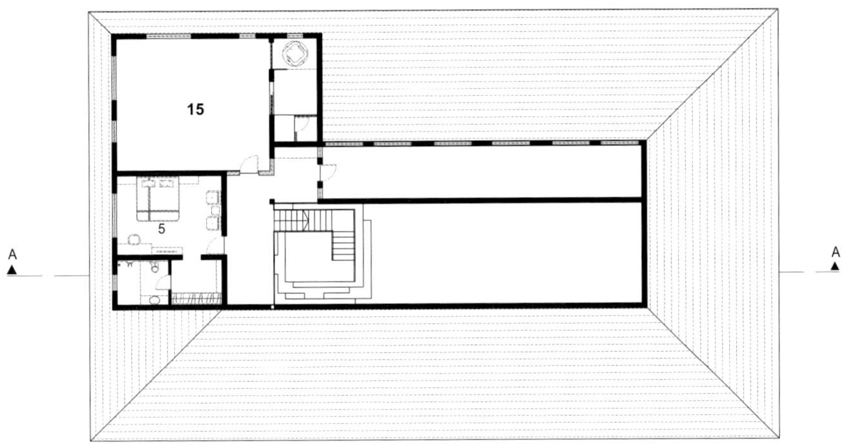

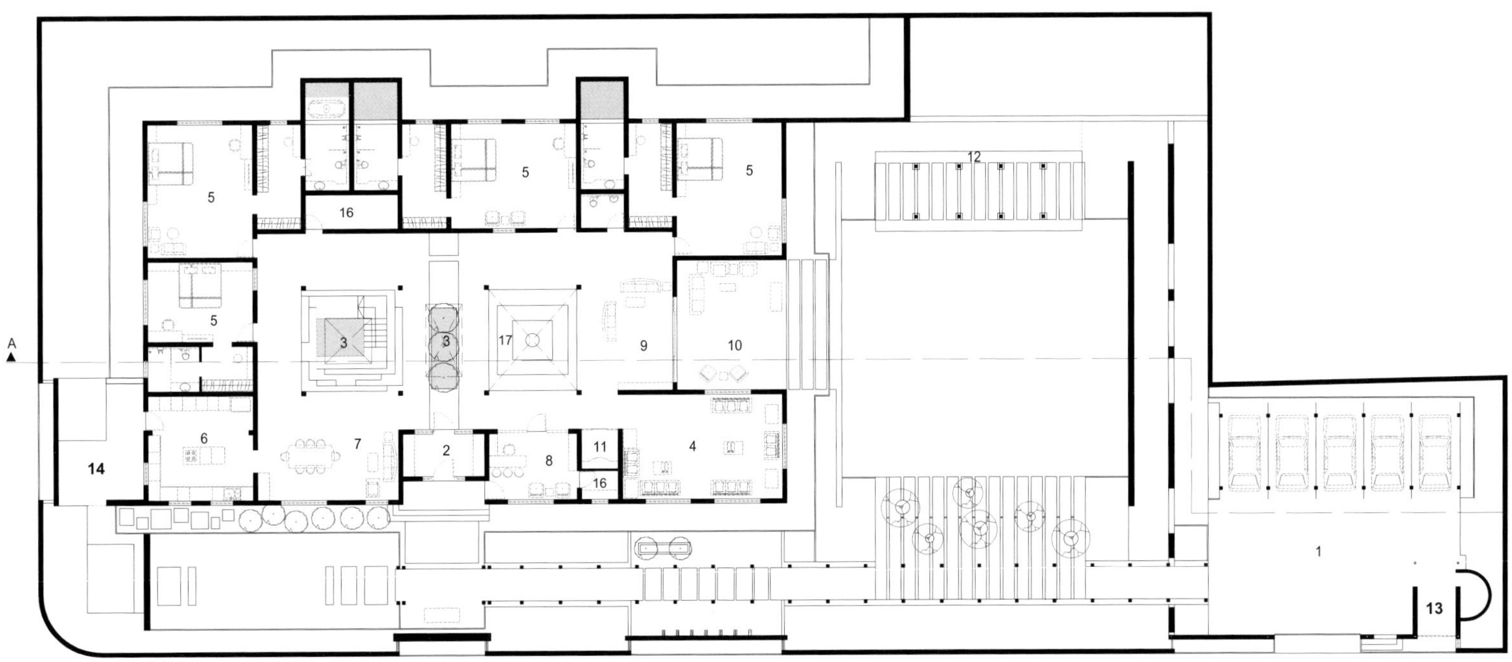

1.PARKING
2.ENTRANCE LOBBY
3.COURTYARD
4.LIVING ROOM
5.BEDROOM
6.KITCHEN
7.DINING
8.STUDY / OFFICE
9.INFORMAL SEATING
10.OUTDOOR SEATING
11.PUJA
12.PAVILLION
13.WATCHMAN'S CABIN
14.UTILITY AREA
15.MULTIPURPOSE ROOM
16.STORE
17. SUNKEN SEATING

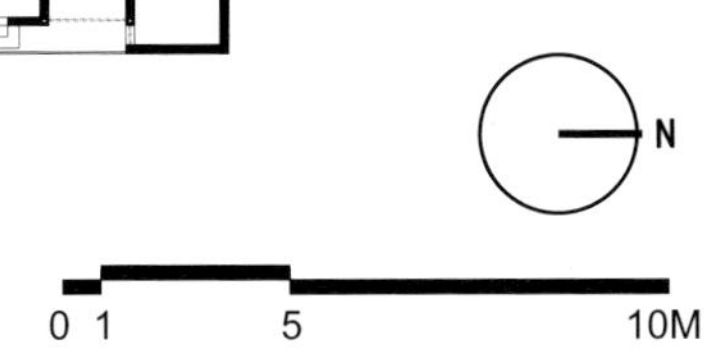

SURYAWANSHI RESIDENCE

2008

Above: The main entrance and canopy designate the line of approach.

In the journey of courtyard houses, this one marks yet another milestone. A non-specific design brief by the client and complete trust in the architect's vision, led to an unhindered design process. The outcome is a space which is contemporary in interpretation yet reflective of the wada topology in its flow of spaces, use of courtyards and natural materials.

The design approach is simple and direct. The main entrance gate and canopy form an off-centre focal point to the structure. From here on it designates the line of approach and a prominent axis that carries across the length of the house. A simple white facade, metal frames and glass cantilevers express a contemporary design vocabulary. In contrast, exposed brick walls in intricate patterns, textured stone and the warm wood lend a rustic touch.

The house is located on a busy street with commercial activities to the south. Thus an inward looking design with a sprawling water court within, gives the needed privacy to the leisure spaces which would otherwise spill over outside the house.

The courtyard is most definitely the dominant feature of the design, merging the backdrop of exposed brick with the still blue water below.

A bridge connects the living and dining spaces through the water, making this short routine movement into an experience.

The spaces are essentially layered in multiple grids, accommodating various activity pockets. The monotony of a regular grid is broken by tilting a major grid at a wide angle, hence carving out interesting volumes within the green spaces and around the open staircase. This skewed grid is reflected again at the entrance adding dynamism and continuity of the concept.

A smaller courtyard in the subsequent grid leads to the private bedrooms at both levels. The dining space in between is lit by wings of skylight from the courtyards on either side. The main courtyard also discreetly continues in the other direction to connect to the pooja room forming a quiet, meditative spot in the midst of other activities. An exposed brick dome embellishes the master bedroom, a demonstration of flawless workmanship by the clients' team of craftsman.

The green spaces gently seep into various portions of the structure letting nature become an inherent part of it. This strong link of the spaces with the earth on one end and the sky at the other, make the spatial experience complete.

Left: The water court provides evaporative and convective cooling.

Left: Exposed brick boundary wall strike a contrast with the main structure.
Right: The dining area surrounded by skylit courtyards.

Page 178, 179: A bridge spanning the water court connects the living and dining space.
Left: The view while transiting the passage.
Right: An exposed brick dome in the master bedroom.

Below: The transition spaces at the upper level overlooking the lower floor.

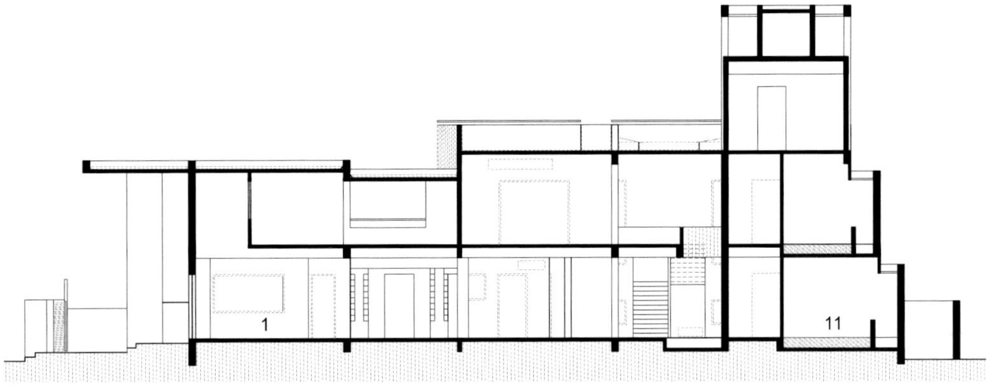

SECTION

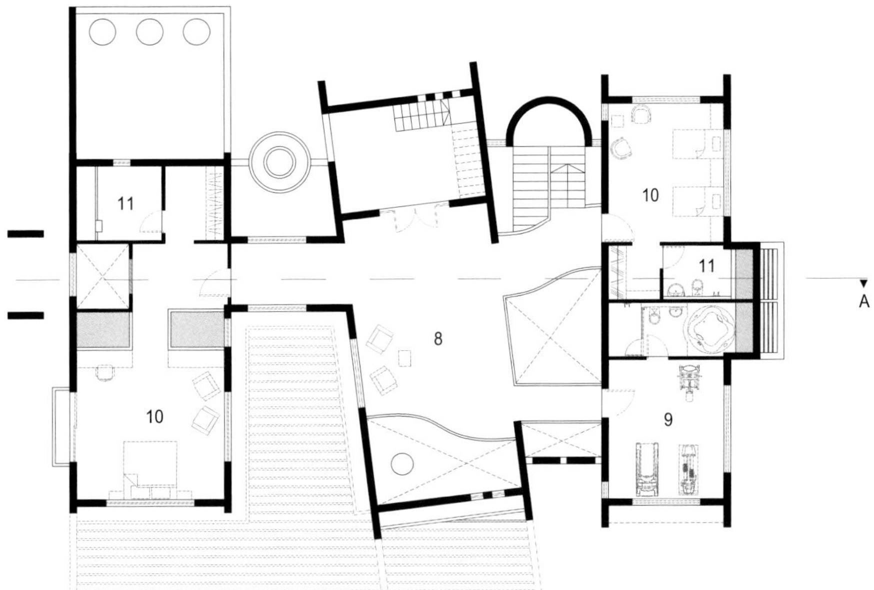

FIRST FLOOR PLAN

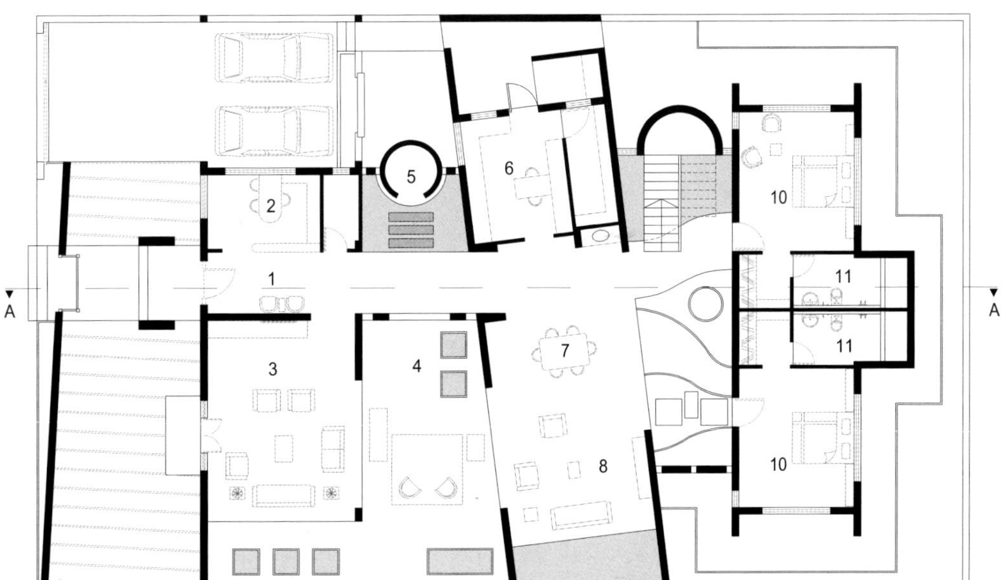

GROUND FLOOR PLAN

A.ENTRANCE LOBBY
B.WORKSPACE
C.LIVING ROOM
D.COURT WITH WATER BODY
E.POOJA ROOM
F.KITCHEN
G.DINING
H.FAMILY SEATING
J.GYMNASIUM
K.BEDROOM
L.TOILET & BATH

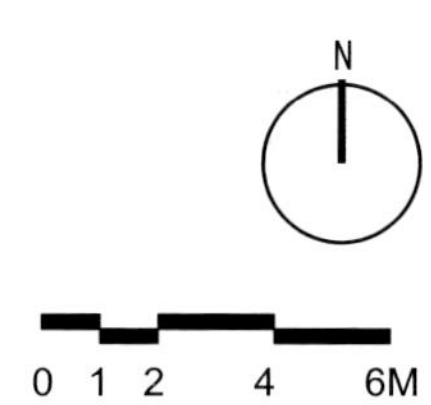

SANDIP FOUNDATION

2008

Located on a twenty-six acre parcel of hilly land on the way to Trimbakeshwar, the Sandip Foundation, College of Engineering campus serves as a microcosm for budding engineers to learn, interact and build memories.

Spaces for learning, interaction and recreation flow in and out of the built form in a rhythmic pattern, creating paths and goals in an alternating repetition. The concept of an open palm is used to evolve the spaces along the contours, with common areas forming the palm and spaces needed for each engineering stream radiating out as five fingers.

A massive curved stone-clad wall emerges out of a raised green mound to define an impressive entrance to the campus. The local stone continues throughout the campus at the ground floor level giving it a distinguished institutional feel and stands out against the smooth plastered finish elsewhere. Most of the stone is quarried from the site itself and used in a coursed manner to impart a sense of discipline.

Solids and voids balance themselves to create formal learning spaces interspersed by open green pockets. This rhythmic pattern of built and unbuilt fans out gracefully, embracing a sprawling central amphitheatre which serves as the

Above: Conical air vents in vibrant china mosaic patterns emerge from the cafeteria below.

geometric and functional centre of the campus and an echo of all the activities held there. A vast sweeping curve deeply interlocks with pure orthogonal forms to give meaning to an awkward shaped site.

Pathways with double height abut trellised green spaces, binding together the various spaces and providing a perfect transition from inside to outside. The patterns thrown by the light and shade are enhanced by use of cement silica fibre board sheets forming horizontal slats creating an envelope around the buildings, providing much needed relief from harsh glare and heavy rains that lash the foothills of the Sahyadris. This detail was also devised to speed up construction as against conventional chajja details. More importantly it separates the structure from the skin, generating a recurring pattern that gives an identity to the campus.

The extent of landscape does not stop outdoors but seeps into the common space within. Classrooms, seminar rooms, labs and other related learning spaces are well lit and well equipped with the latest facilities and thermal comfort. Splashes of colour accentuated by daylight lend life and cheer to the internal spaces. North facing glazing drenches the space in daylight whilst

Left: The curved stone-clad wall defines the entrance of the campus.
Right: The north facing glazing lets in diffused light.

eliminating glare and heat.

The earth sheltered cafeteria forms another functional centre of the campus, with young minds always flocking into this hidden retreat for food and recreation. The amphitheater enclosed within, is a natural spill over to the space encouraging interaction and brainstorming activities. Spaces emerge from the earth in tandem with the natural slope and with minimal intervention into the existing contours. Conical mechanical exhaust vents finished in vibrant china mosaic patterns pierce the green roof adding sculptural elements to the landscape.

A college campus plays an important role in a student's formative phase of life. The sensitively designed campus for Sandip Foundation, College of Engineering goes a long way in creating an environment that provides comfort, fun and nurturing to many young and fertile minds.

Right: North facing lobby with patches of green.

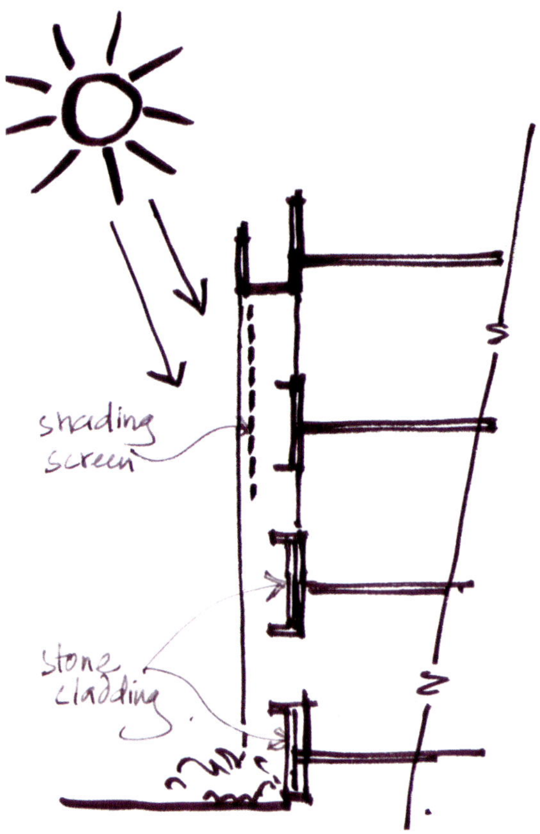
shading
screen
stone
cladding

Page 190, 191: Covered pathways with double height abutting green spaces on either side.
Bottom: The sprawling amphitheatre into which the built spaces converge.

Page 194, 195: Horizontal slats envelope the buildings protecting against harsh glare.
Page 196, 197: The covered transition spaces spilling over into the central landscaped area.
Above: Intermediate patches of green link the built space.

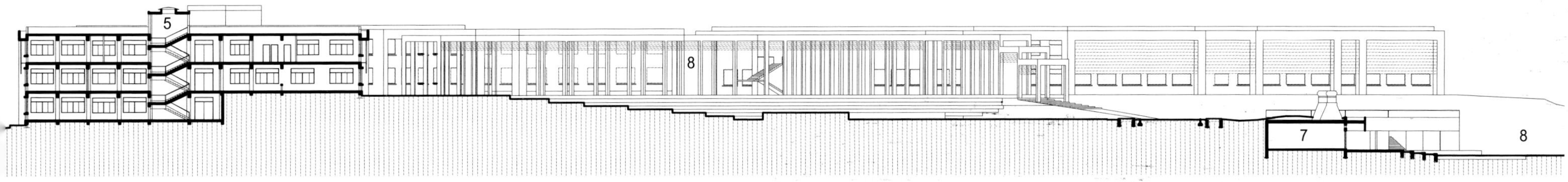

SECTION - AA'

0 5 10 20 30M

1.ENTRANCE LOBBY
2.ADMINISTRATION
3.LIBRARY
4.LABORATORIES
5.ACADEMIC BLOCK
6.WORKSHOP
7.CANTEEN
8.TERRACE
9.AMPHITHEATER

N

SITE PLAN

0 5 10 20 30M

WORKSPACE FOR MR. BHUJBAL

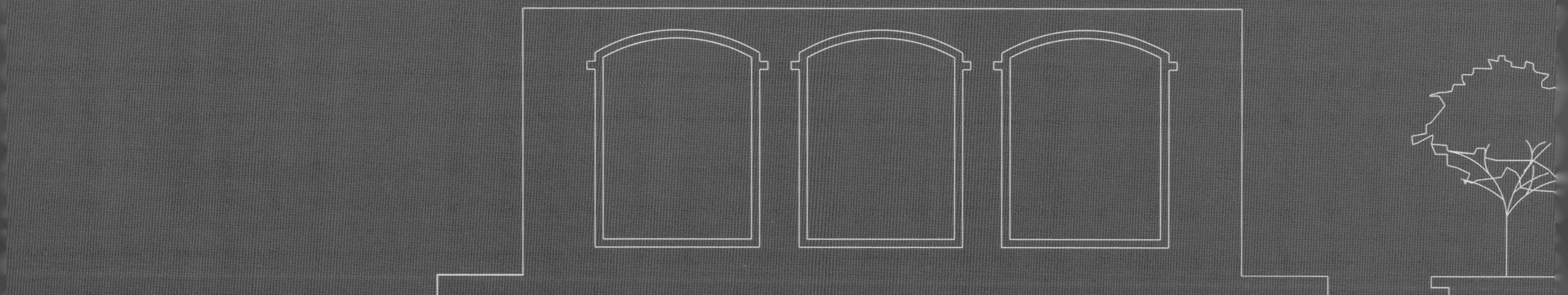

2009

This is a workspace far removed from the stereotype formality and sterility that a typical office culture exudes. This is a power center that attracts a huge number of visitors at any point of time. It was imperative that the architectural vocabulary should make a strong statement to every person who steps into it.

The architect has used the language of restrained elegance to create this impact. Nestled on a sizeable piece of land, the campus conveys the ease of an office spread across one level. Given the clients' liking for colonial architecture, the design is reminiscent of architecture of that era, not just in aspects of detailing but also scale and proportions of spaces. A major influence comes from a heritage resort in Matheran, whose verandas were documented and used by the architect to develop this design.

The entrance itself is striking, as a carpet of lush landscape sets a beautiful foreground to the main structure. A water pool surrounds the reception area, creating reflections that doubles the impact and also forms a barrier to control movement of individuals and groups. The semi-enclosed reception space comfortably holds a large number of visitors at a time.

Above: Generous transitional spaces with customised terrazzo flooring.

The space planning is extremely logical and simple, with two wings of colonnaded workspaces wrapped around the central reception area. This common space is the heart of the design; clearly the functional and visual focus of the space. This space is connected to the rest of the area through bridges at the extreme end of the wings. Generous roof slopes organically relate to the building grid.

Sprawling transitional areas blend the spaces into each other creating a sense of continuity and unity within the office. Customised terrazzo flooring in earthy colours, timber detailing and handcrafted textiles add nostalgia. Intricate wrought iron railings, stone and metal artefacts, light fixtures and fans echo the past.

Despite the highly crafted detailing and the elaborate style of architecture, there is a strong undercurrent of restraint in the way this style is expressed; making the design comfortable and easy on the eye.

Right : Extensive landscape surrounds the built spaces.

Page 204 Top: Intricate detailing in wrought iron and timber.
Page 204 Bottom: A water body creates a boundary around the structure.
Page 205: Visual relief provided by ample daylight and green spaces.
Left: The spacious cabin space with a colonial touch.
Right: A glimpse of the connecting verandas.

Left: Detailing of plinth to give a floating effect.
Right: Ample foreground gives a perspective.

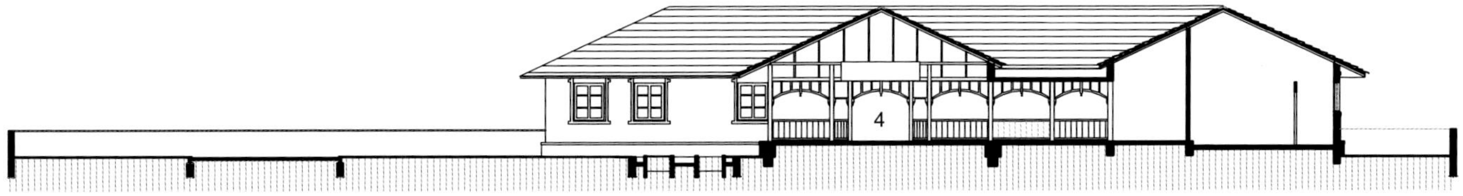

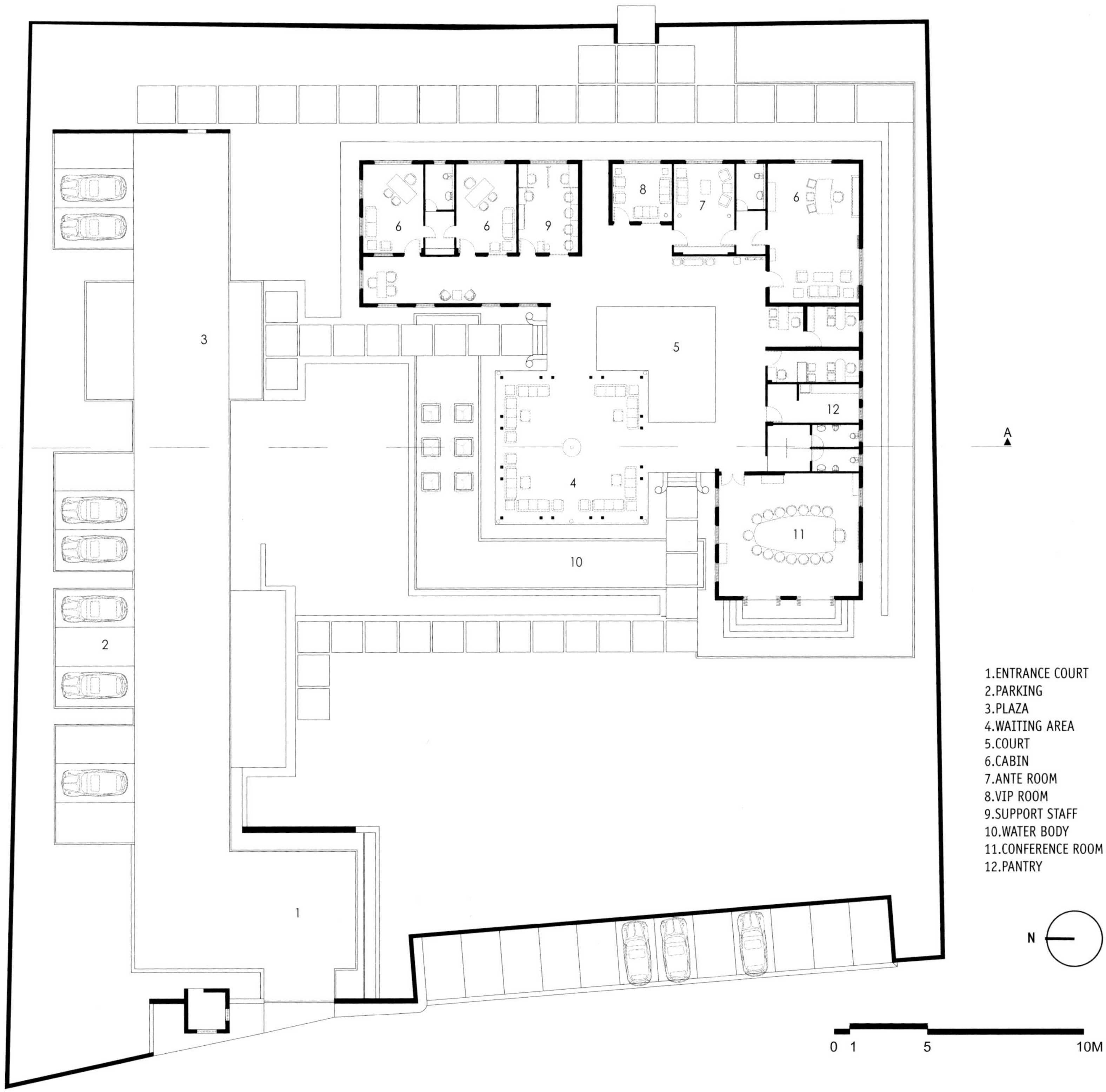

Left: The board room sheltered by a sloping roof.

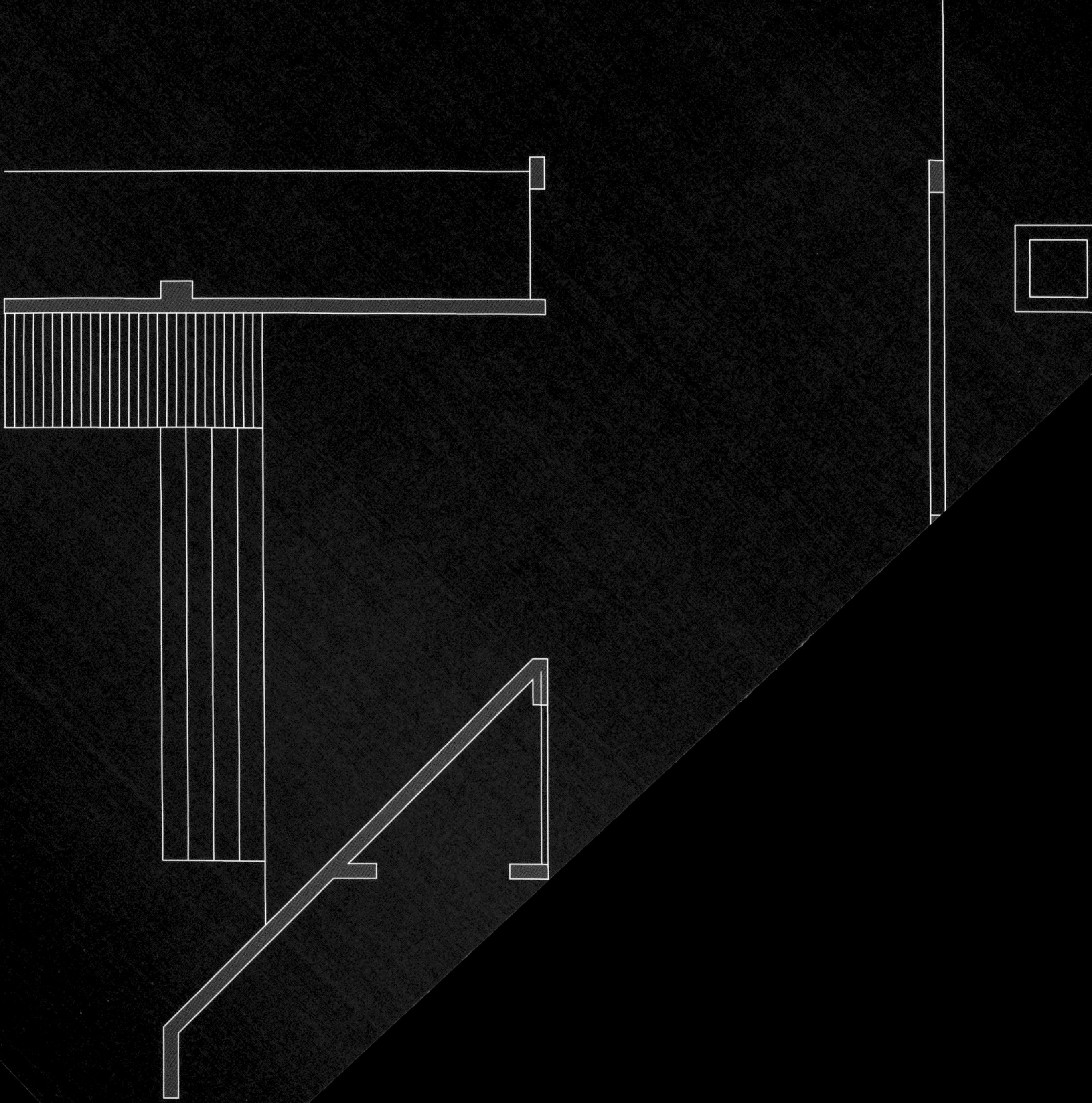

Vineyards have always been integral to the identity of Nashik, a visual treat to visitors and locals alike. However, living in the middle of a vineyard and experiencing it at close quarters is a unique experience. Nestled in the midst of a vineyard, the Beyond Resort offers its users one such experience.

On the outskirts of the city, the main entrance to the property emerges in the midst of a vineyard, leading to a cluster of units in serene white. Located on the highest contour of the land, all guest rooms get an uninterrupted view of the vineyard with an infinity pool in the foreground and a dam in the background. The vocabulary of design is unpretentious, yet luring the visitor into its fold; the pristine white emerging as a contrast against the green surrounds.

The quiet entrance tucked behind an unembellished wall takes the visitor by surprise as it opens generously into the reception lounge. A band of wooden jali provides shade whilst throwing interesting shadows around. As one transitions into the double-height lobby, a wooden bridge leads you over a water body to a landscaped courtyard that forms the heart of the space.

Above : Water cascades aiding evaporative cooling.

Left: The landscaped courtyard forming the visual focal point.

Left : Glimpses of green and patterns of daylight add life to the connecting passage.
Right : A glimpse of the guest rooms overlooking the vineyards.

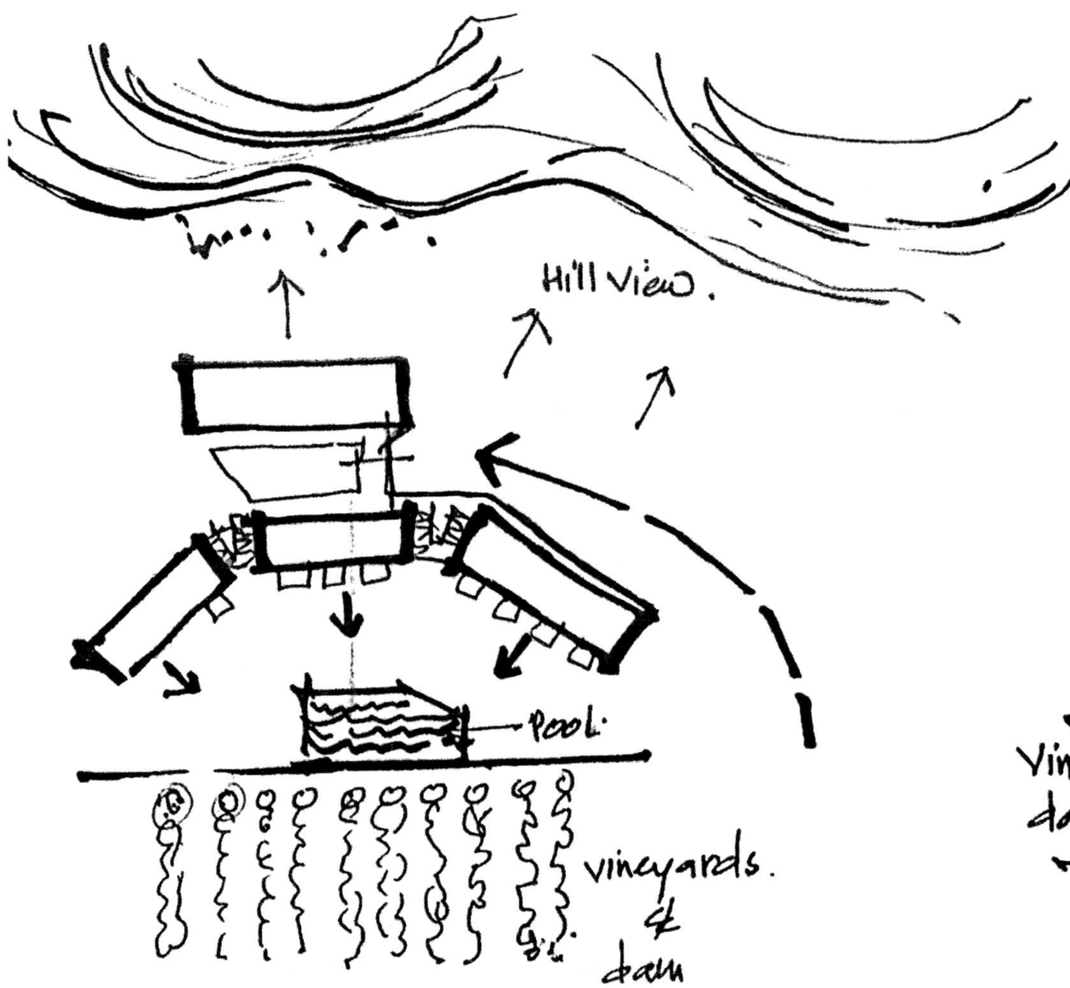
Hill view.
Pool.
vineyards.
&
dam

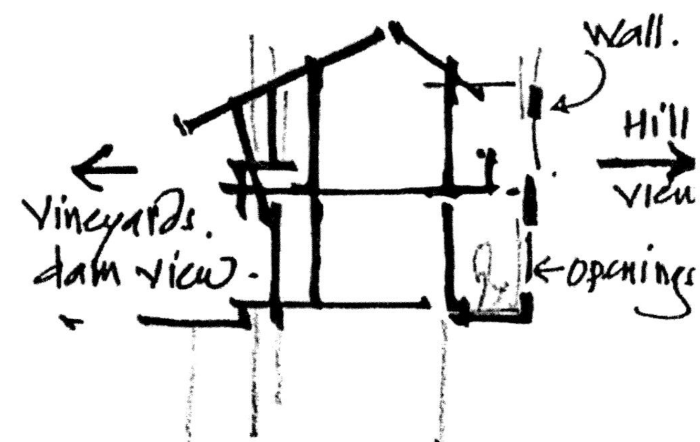
wall.
Hill
view
Vineyards.
dam view.
openings

The pool of light that it creates soothes the entire surrounding and links the common spaces visually. Mounds of green, together with sculptural champa trees, collaborate to cool down the space.

Conceived by the client as a boutique hotel targeted to promote wine tourism in the country, the property has grown from an initial count of twelve rooms to thirty-two in number after completion. The guest rooms are sheltered by sloping roofs with spaces spilling over into deep sit outs that overlook the vineyard. Two layers of metal sheets sandwiched with insulating PUF forms the roof, restricting the intense solar radiation and maintains thermal comfort inside.

The sit outs and the restaurant extend into the pool area surrounded by minimalist landscape forming spaces to meet, relax and enjoy the vineyards that provide a natural boundary to the overall space. A double-height landscaped stretch along the passage area provides a vertical link and the thoughtfully designed punctures frame the view of the ever changing landscape outside.

Structural steel members frame the units, exposing the enhanced column connections and the roofing system. The alternating repetition of the cluster forms an interesting skyline against the natural unhindered setting. The changing colours of the sky at different times of the day bring out the various vibes of the resort; serene and unassuming in daylight and tantalizing and mysterious by sunset.

Truth in detailing, subtlety in use of material and sensitive space planning instil a sense of harmony with the site and surrounds. The design philosophy clearly leans towards providing an experience of rejuvenation and oneness with nature, rather than the typically expected forms of ostentatious luxury. All this adds up to making the experience here truly 'beyond' expectations.

Page 222,223: The infinity pool and beyond.
Page 224,225: The deep sit-outs with exposed structural members forming a pattern.

Left: The restaurant connecting to the pool.
Right: Reflections in the pool double the impact.

SULA

Below: The quiet entrance tucked deep into the site.

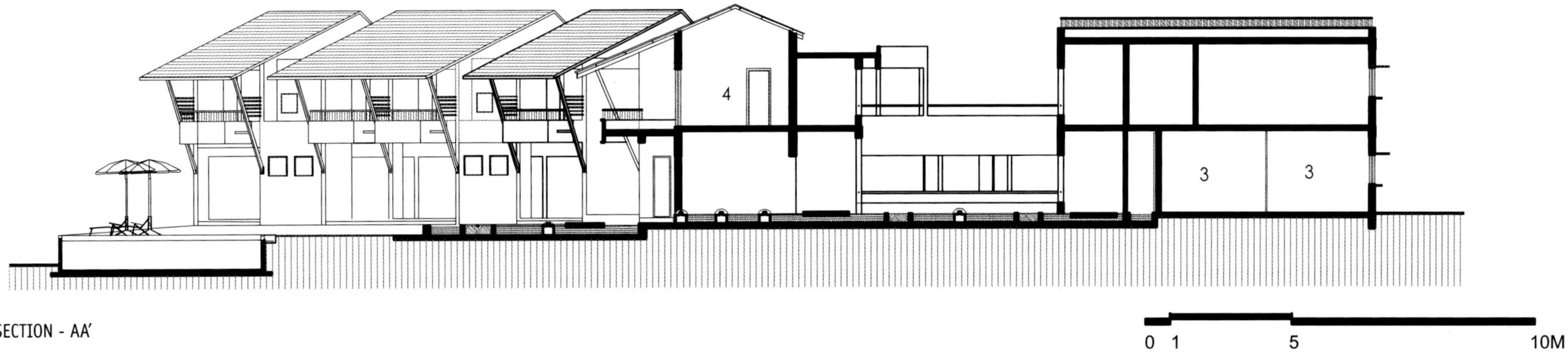

SECTION - AA'

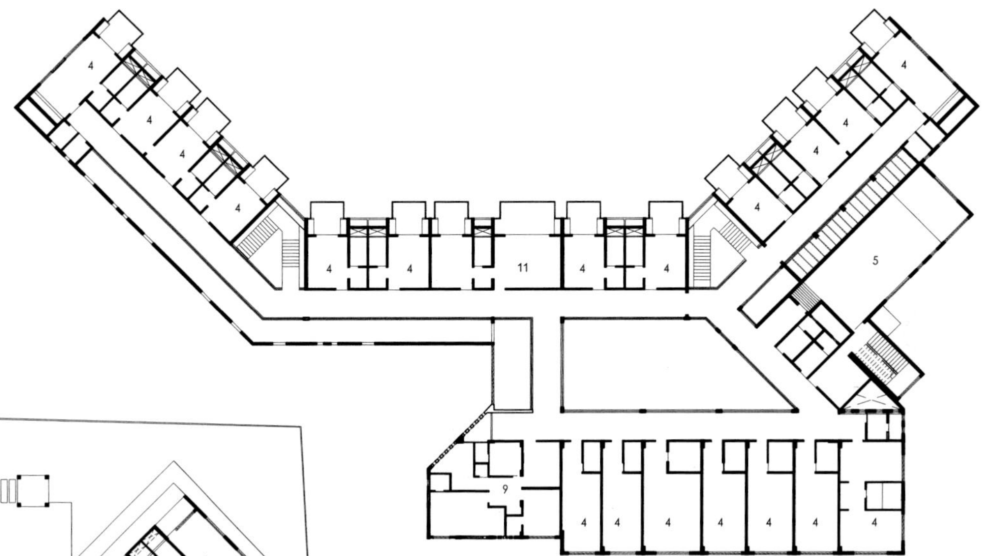

FIRST FLOOR PLAN

FIRST FLOOR PLAN

1.ENTRANCE LOBBY
2.WINE SHOP
3.OFFICE
4.GUEST ROOM
5.GYMNASIUM
6.RESTAURANT
7.KITCHEN
8.SERVICE / STAFF / FACILITY
9.SWIMMING POOL
10.SPA
11.SUITES

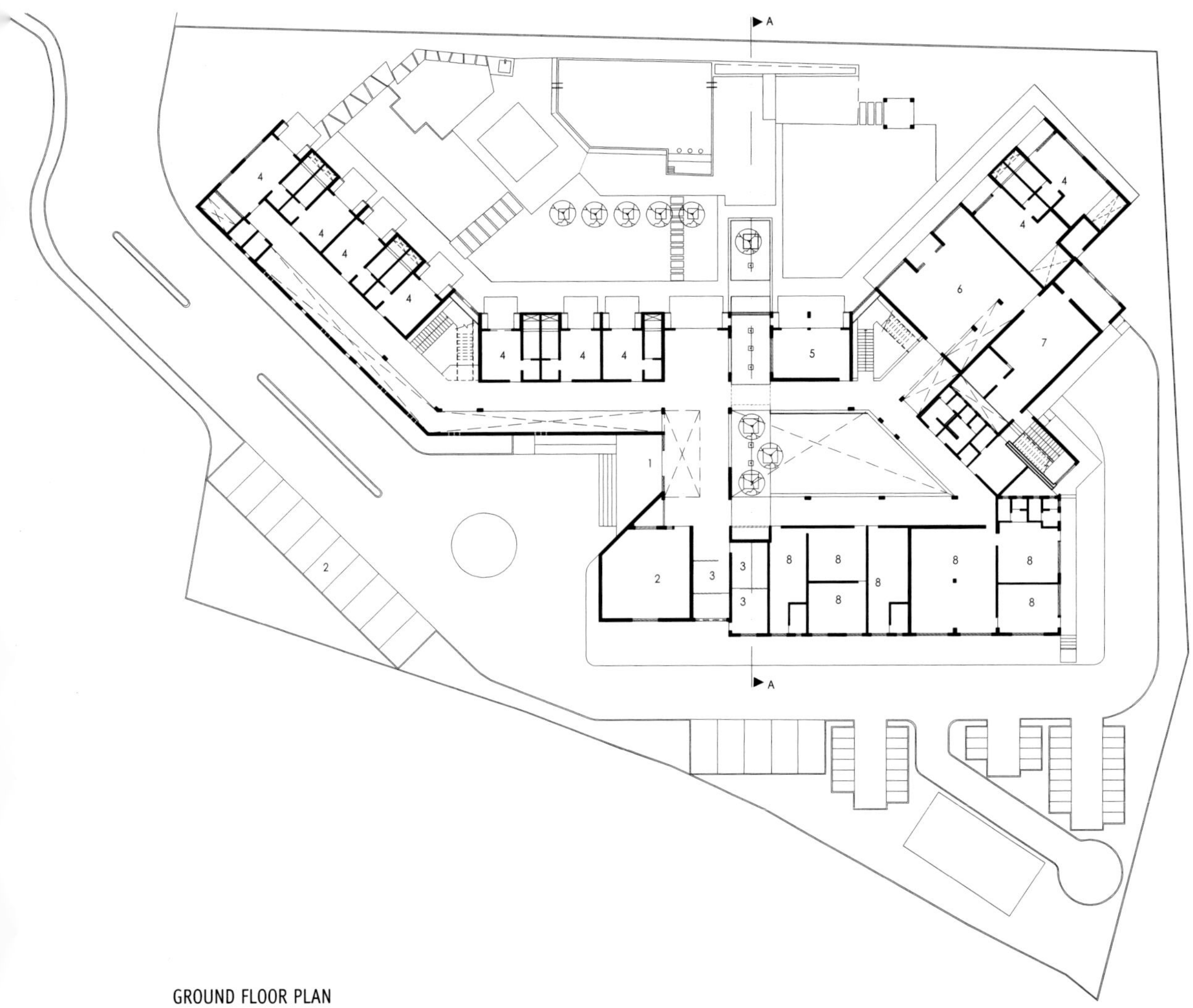

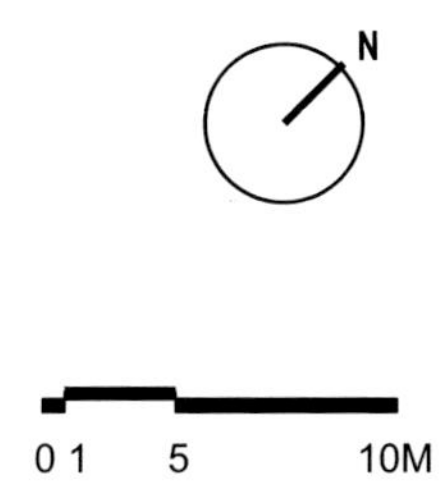

GROUND FLOOR PLAN

YCMOU LIBRARY

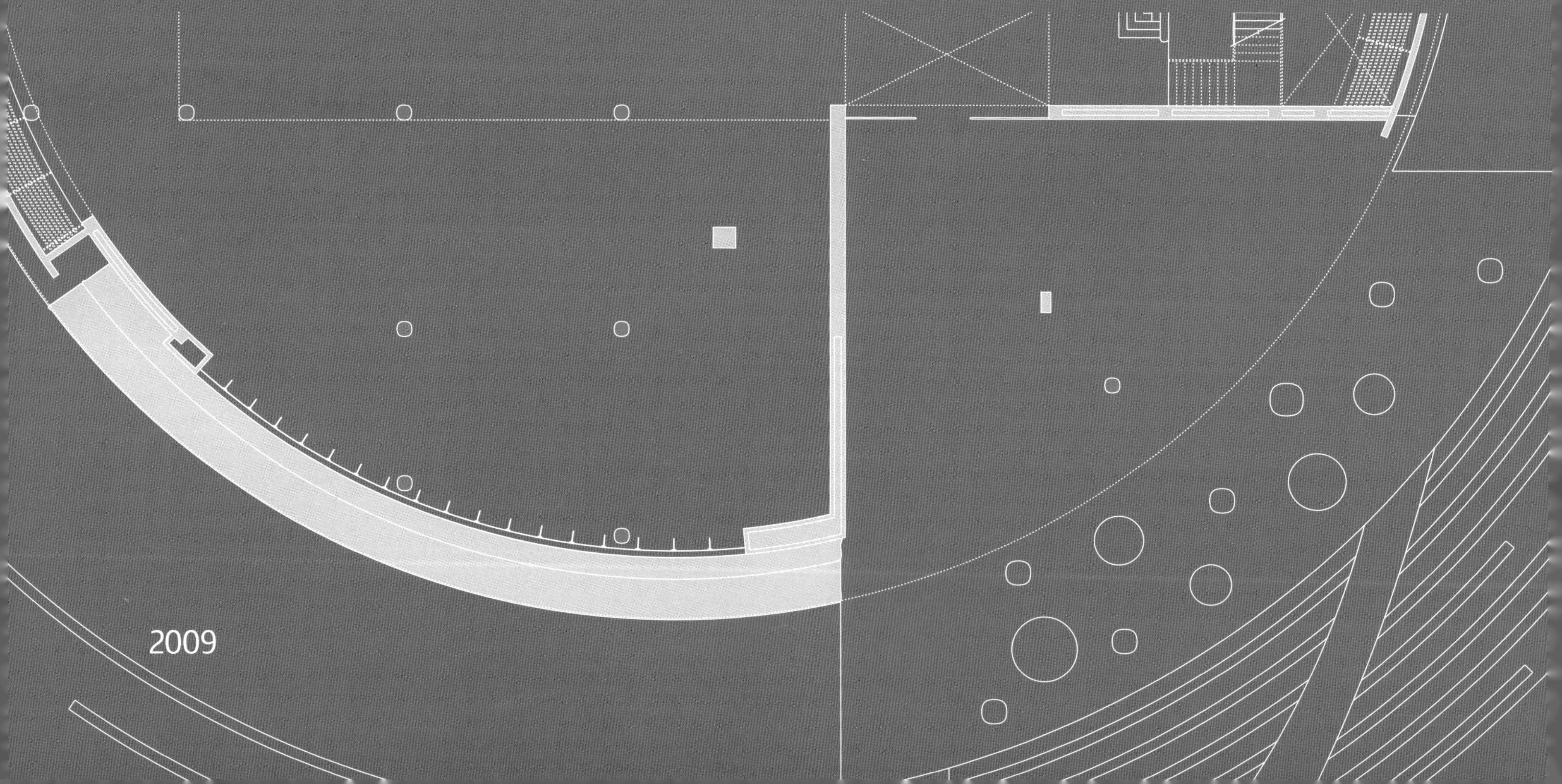

2009

Above: Louvers control natural light and air entering the space.

At the end of a long path within the sprawling YCMOU campus stands a solitary sculptural form housing the library block. Set against the foreground of a generous expanse of lush lawns this lone building and the backdrop of the sky is simple yet striking. A library is symbolic of knowledge and learning. The iconic form of this structure ensures that it fulfils this important need of the client brief and gives it its due prominence in the campus.

Set on a contoured site, the building is defined by an imaginary boundary created by a series of free-flowing curvilinear lawn clad steps. As one strolls along these, you can feel the rhythm of the layers flow further down the site as it follows the natural slope and culminates into an amphitheater A visual balance is created between the massive built form of the library and the activity center outside.

The library building itself is derived from a pure circular form, layered to create multiple boundaries around the periphery of the building. The louvers, overhangs and other shading devices formed in these layers are derived from a sun-path analysis of the building and site. The chamfered, insulated light roof, slopes gracefully towards the north like a sun dial and reduces heat gain in the spaces below.

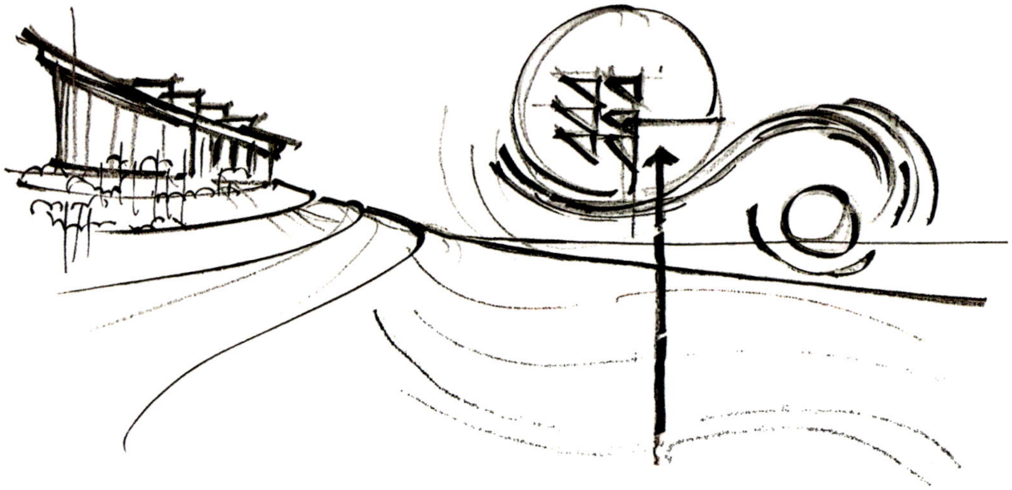

It also eases down the volume and the structural load of the roof. The clerestory openings with mechanical extractors poised on top of the insulated metal roof create patterns.

The entrance lobby is carved out by subtracting a volume from the cylinder, making it prominent. The levels within the library space follow the site gradient. Once inside, one finds that the spaces are lit by the large patch of north light glazing. These supplemented by the openings in the roof create wings of light. The diffused north light as a primary light source with minimal openings otherwise, provides ample natural light for the primary activity of reading.

As you transition from the outdoors to the library inside, one cannot fail to notice the significant drop in temperature. The mechanical air extractors work ceaselessly to create a convective current and ventilate a large volume naturally. Internal courtyards provide vertical links between floors and assist in the stack ventilation.

Respect to the existing architecture within the campus is demonstrated by continuity in the external surface texture. In a simple approach, the design is guided by the natural features of the site, climatic needs and a sustainable approach to design. Use of pure forms enhanced by meticulous detailing and generosity of daylight, make it a compelling structure visually and a comfortable space internally.

Page 230: The first glimpse of the solitary structure as one approaches the entrance.
Left: The sculptural form is accentuated in the night.

Left: Clerestory openings with mechanical extractors creating a rhythm.
Right: The insulated lightweight roof bringing in diffused north light.
Page 236: The form of the amphitheatre respects the natural contour and balances the built form.

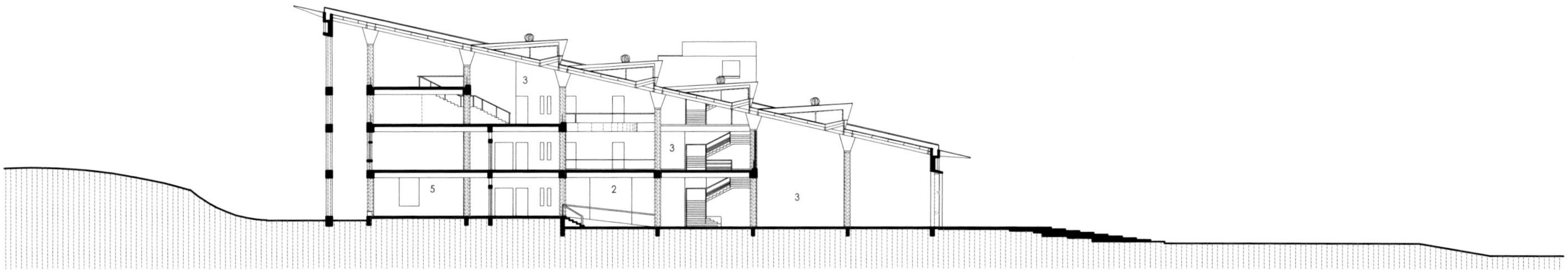

SECTION - AA'

1.ENTRANCE PLAZA
2.WAITING AREA
3.BOOKS STACKING / READING AREA
4.BOOK STORE
5.ADMINISTRATION
6.AV ROOM
7.AMPHITHEATER
8.GREEN ROOM / PUBLIC TOILET

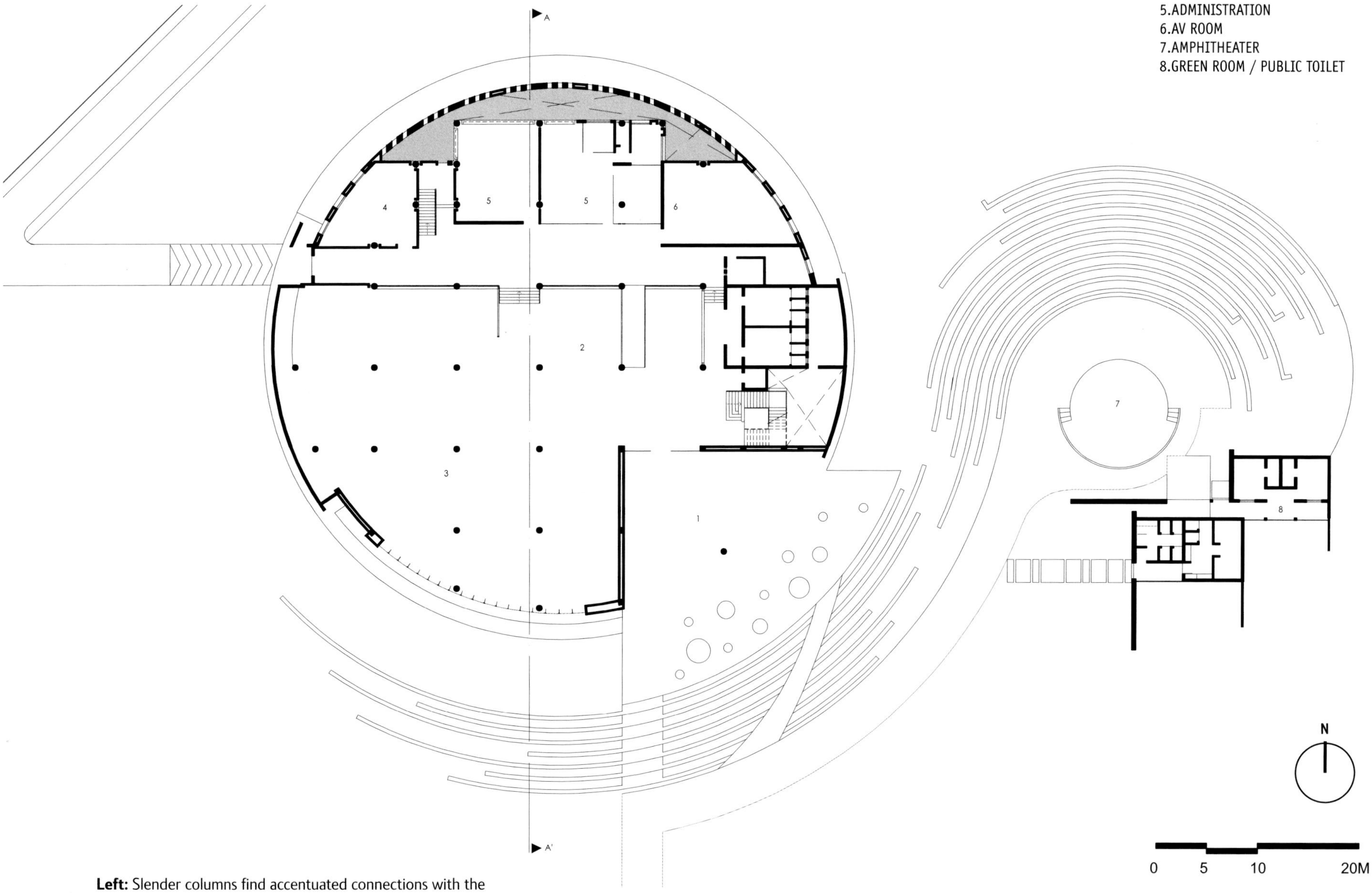

Left: Slender columns find accentuated connections with the roof.

GROUND FLOOR PLAN

ADAPTIVE REUSE - PAPAYA NURSERY

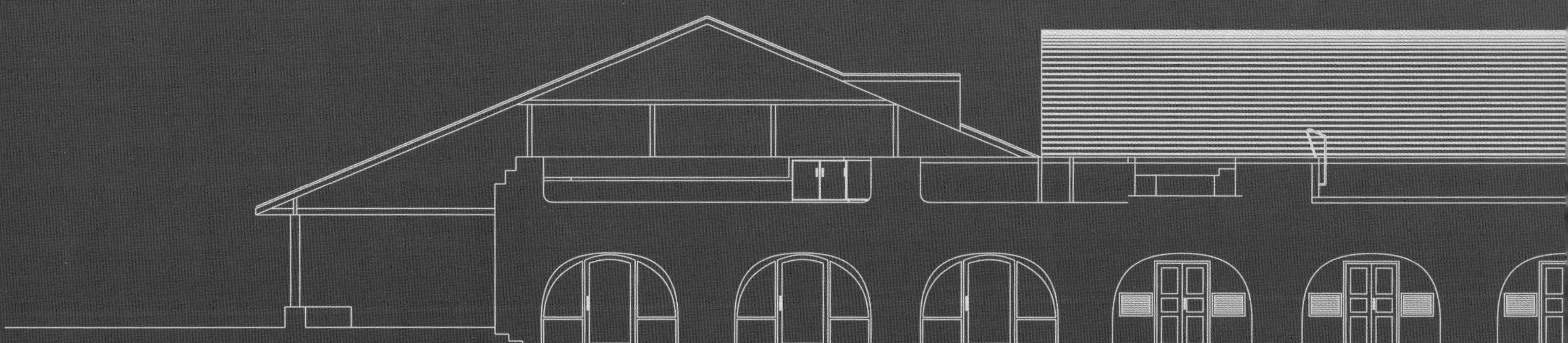

2011

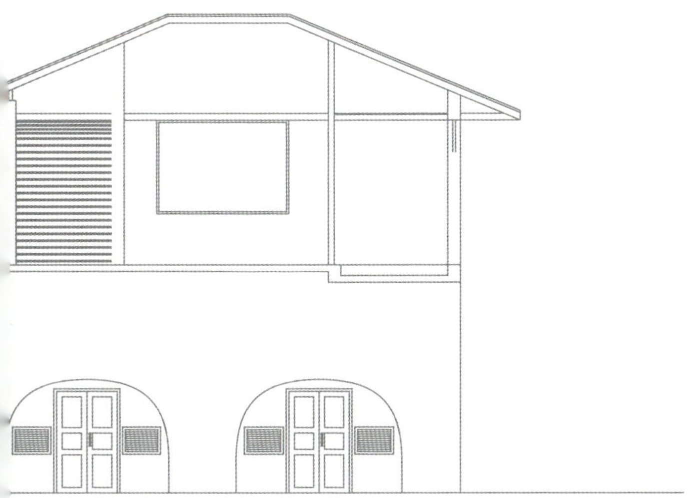

Above: A glimpse from the poolside.

Adaptive reuse of a structure has always been viewed as a sensitive approach to architecture. Respect for existing architecture and the energy saving achieved by retaining the building shell make the effort truly worthwhile.

It is hard to imagine that the serene and intimate office space for Papaya Nursery was originally built in the British era as a military bunker with water reservoirs above it. The land was in possession of the client since 1932 and one out of the four bunkers finally remained. The architect and client saw potential in this site, its vaults and water tanks and visualized a better use of the existing spaces.

The story which began with just the need of an overhang to protect the structure against the rains went on to creating a beautiful transition space and way beyond. Retaining the existing structure was a non-negotiable criterion for both the client and the architect.

Having known the client for over twenty years meant that the architect deeply understood their lifestyle and working of the office.

Today, the eight vaulted voids in the bunkers have been converted into flexible work spaces, meeting hubs and service areas. The sheltered waiting space around it creates the transition path

Left: The existing structure photographed in 1995.
Right: The deep veranda sheltering the new workspace.

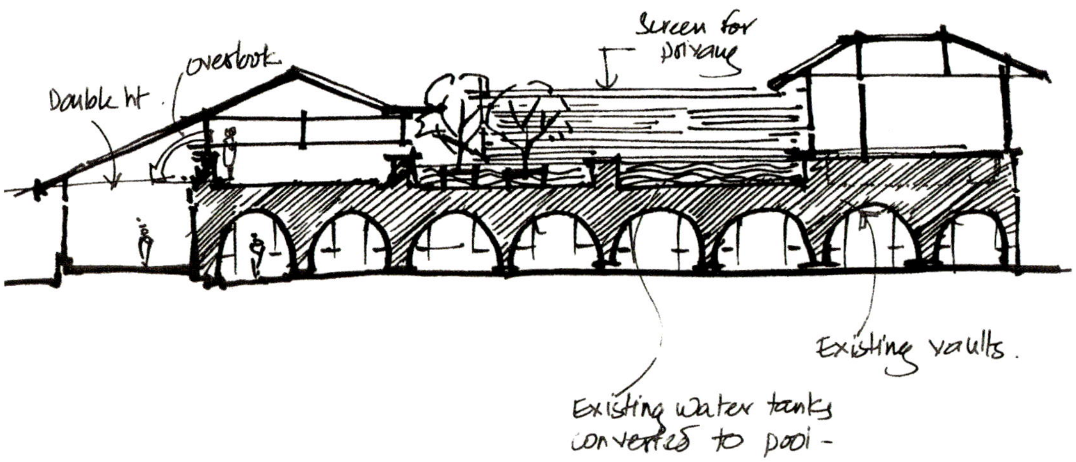

connecting the activity pockets to the vast green earth mounds beyond.

The form of the vault creates natural doors and windows and lends a rhythm to the facade outside. White rough cast plaster imparts an appealing texture to the surfaces. Finer details like retention of old ladders and an existing well, echo its historic past. Water from the well is recycled for watering the nursery, with the well itself being converted into a fountain that humidifies the air and provides a visual treat.

The entire structure is sheltered by a massive sloping roof that envelopes the existing structure and protects it. The existing voids of the erstwhile water reservoirs have been converted into a covered seating space, a swimming pool, and guest rooms. As one ascends the open stairs to the upper level, the serene pool is a sure element of surprise. A bridge over the pool connects restrooms with the covered seating serving as an axis between the covered spaces.

The intimacy gradient has been sensitively worked out with public, semi-private and private spaces co-existing in the same setting. Use of cement fibre sheets for roofs, railings and screens create continuity in the design expression. Exposed wire-cut bricks form a garden wall that protects the solitude of the space from sights and sounds of the busy road outside.

The entire campus has a secretive quality about it. The structure resonates with intrigue and history of an era gone by, yet blending beautifully with the modern day needs of a work cum leisure space.

Left: The structure and surrounds after restoration.

Page 246: The bridge connects the gathering area to the swimming pool.
Page 247: A privacy screen using a pattern of cement fibre sheets.
Bottom: A massive sloping roof that envelops the entire structure.

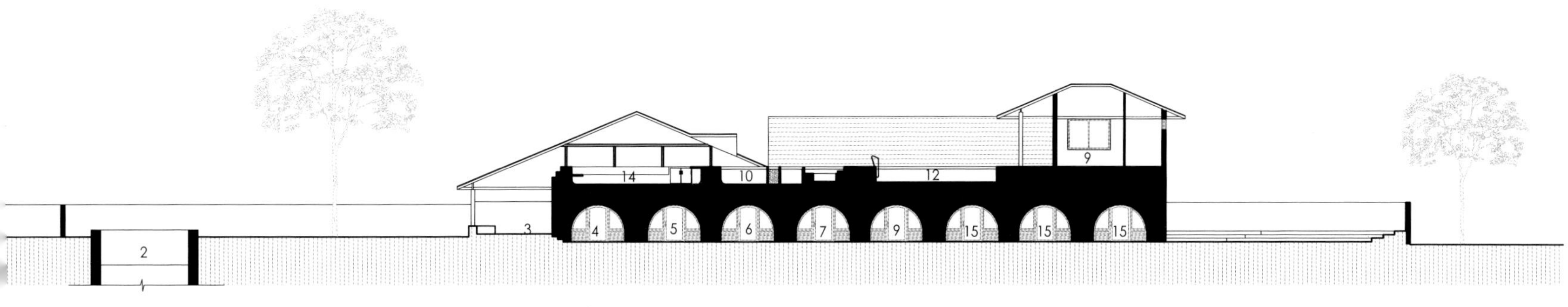

SECTION AA

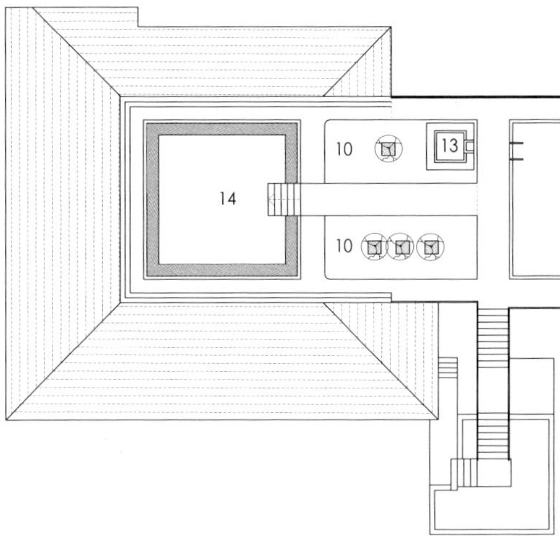

FIRST FLOOR PLAN

1.ENTRANCE FOYER
2.WELL
3.COVERED SEATING
4.EXECUTIVE CABIN
5.MEETING ROOM
6.KITCHEN & RESTROOM
7.STORE ROOM
8.FILTRATION PLANT
9.BEDROOM
10.WATER BODY
11.AMPHITHEATER
12.SWIMMING POOL
13.JACUZZI
14.FAMILY SEATING
15.OFFICE AREA

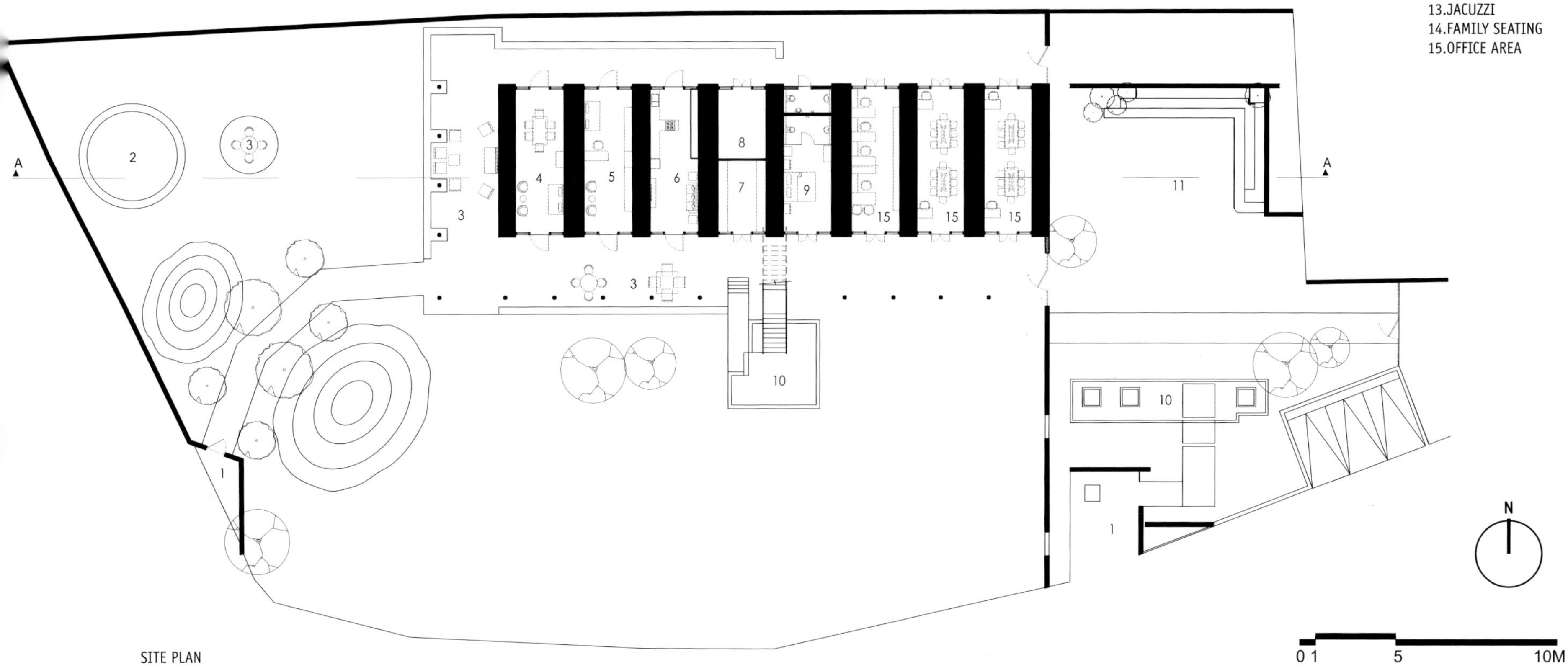

SITE PLAN

WORKSPACE FOR GREEN SPACE REALTORS

2012

Above: The main entrance defined by wooden pergolas and splashes of green.

Every project provides its own set of challenges. The measure of good design is in seeing these challenges as opportunities and converting them into merits of the project. This design for a developer's office space was one such new challenge, where the project constraints have been used positively to produce sustainable architecture.

The office is designed on a compact site located in the midst of the new business center of Nashik. The site housed an existing building shell built to accommodate multiple dwellings at each level with a common boundary wall. The client expressed a leaning towards sustainable design which extends from his personal liking to his business philosophy.

Being totally in sync with the architect's outlook, the plan started out with an attempt to salvage the entire structure. However, with several constraints due to change of use, finally the existing basement was retained and remodeled to accommodate a water tank, hence reducing on energy used to demolish and rebuild the space.

The design builds its way around the very basic philosophy of 'respect for environment' and finds its answers in amazing ways. Simplicity in space planning clubbed with openness and vertical connections, makes the compact volume appear generous.

The main entrance moves along the axis of the garden wall meticulously patterned in fly-ash and terra cotta wire-cut bricks, creating shadows on its surface which help avoid heat gain. Open grid pavement for the parking spots allows the ground to breathe. Doors, windows and furniture are made out of reclaimed wood. The visual and tactile feel of natural materials adds warmth and comfort.

Daylight filtering through the foliage of existing trees reduces glare. The common building edge houses a stretch of courtyards within, providing natural light and visual relief to the cabin spaces. Mechanical turbo ventilators help extract the hot air and generate a stack effect.

The existing basement is used for rain water harvesting. This water is recycled through pipes under the floor surface to provide radiant cooling to the building. Modern and traditional methods of passive cooling are harmoniously integrated through the design. Use of LED lights reduces the energy consumption to a great extent. Low VOC paints and adhesives eliminate health hazards to the occupants and the site team.

While being functionally distinct, this building tells a story of how sincerity of purpose can find its way through every constraint; that sustainability can be infused into every design and good intent always finds a route to its fulfilment.

Right: A tranquil water body at the rear end, adding to the evaporative cooling.

Above left and right: Vertical connections open out the compact spaces.
Right: The single stringer staircase with a mural creating a focal point.

Left: The board room and beyond.
Right: Open office layout allows daylight to penetrate.

Left: An enclosed workspace with a light well at the rear.
Right: The head's cabin with furniture crafted from reclaimed wood.

GREEN
SPACES
REALTORS

SECTION AA

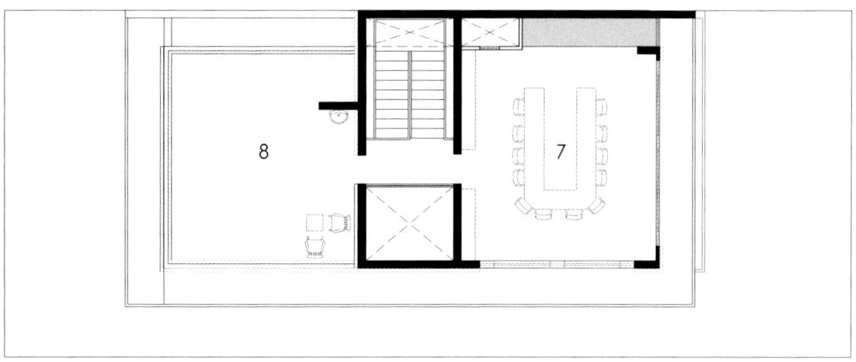

SECOND FLOOR PLAN

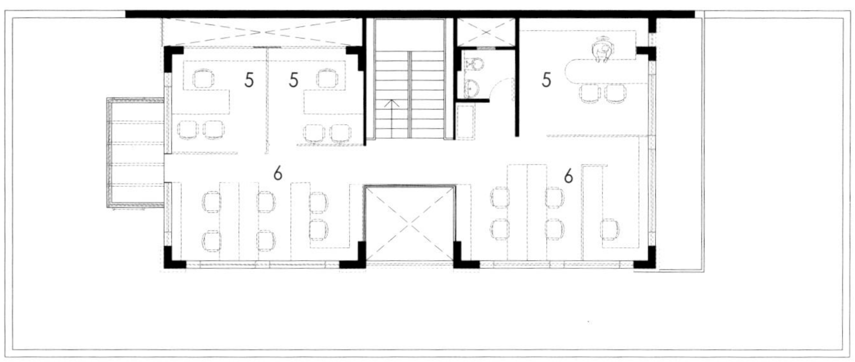

FIRST FLOOR PLAN

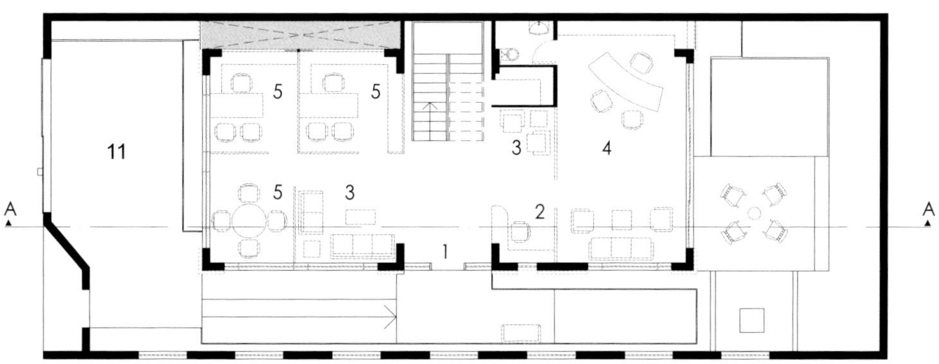

Left: A view from the flanking street.

GROUND FLOOR PLAN

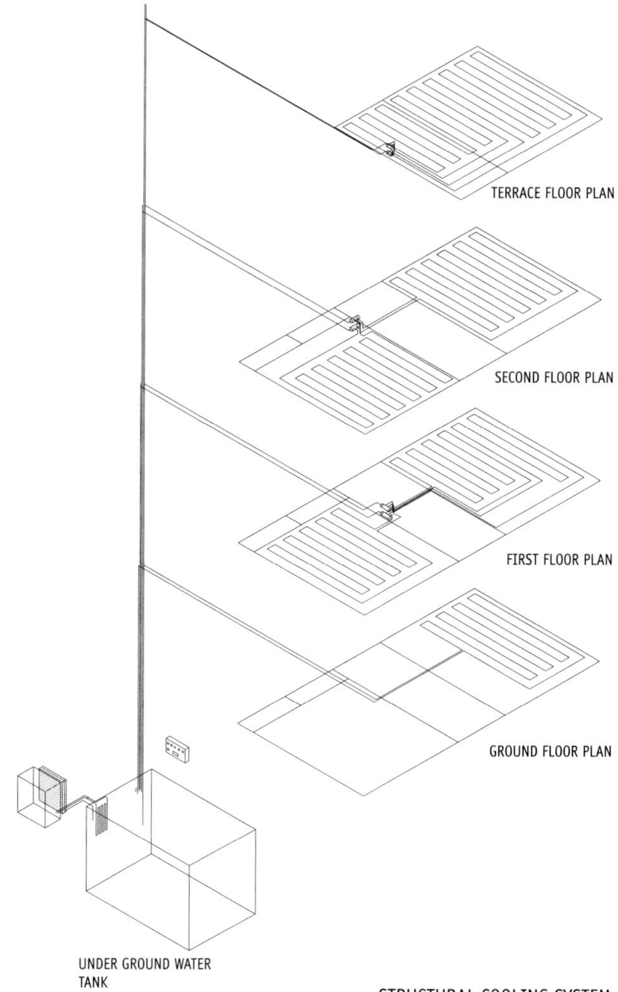

STRUCTURAL COOLING SYSTEM WITH CIRCULATING WATER.

1.ENTRANCE LOBBY
2.RECEPTION
3.WAITING
4.HEAD'S CABIN
5.CABIN
6.STAFF
7.CONFERENCE ROOM
8.TERRACE
9.UNDERGROUND WATER TANK FOR DOMESTIC USE
10.RAINWATER HARVESTING TANK & STRUCTURAL COOLING SYSTEM
11.PARKING

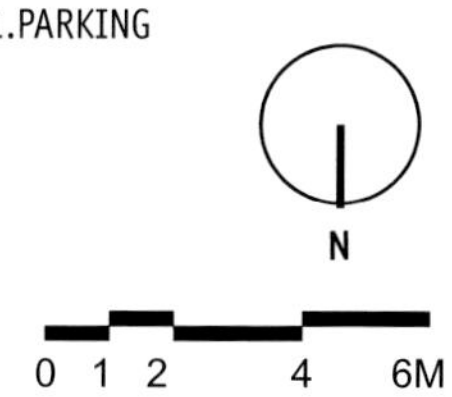

BAGAD RESIDENCE

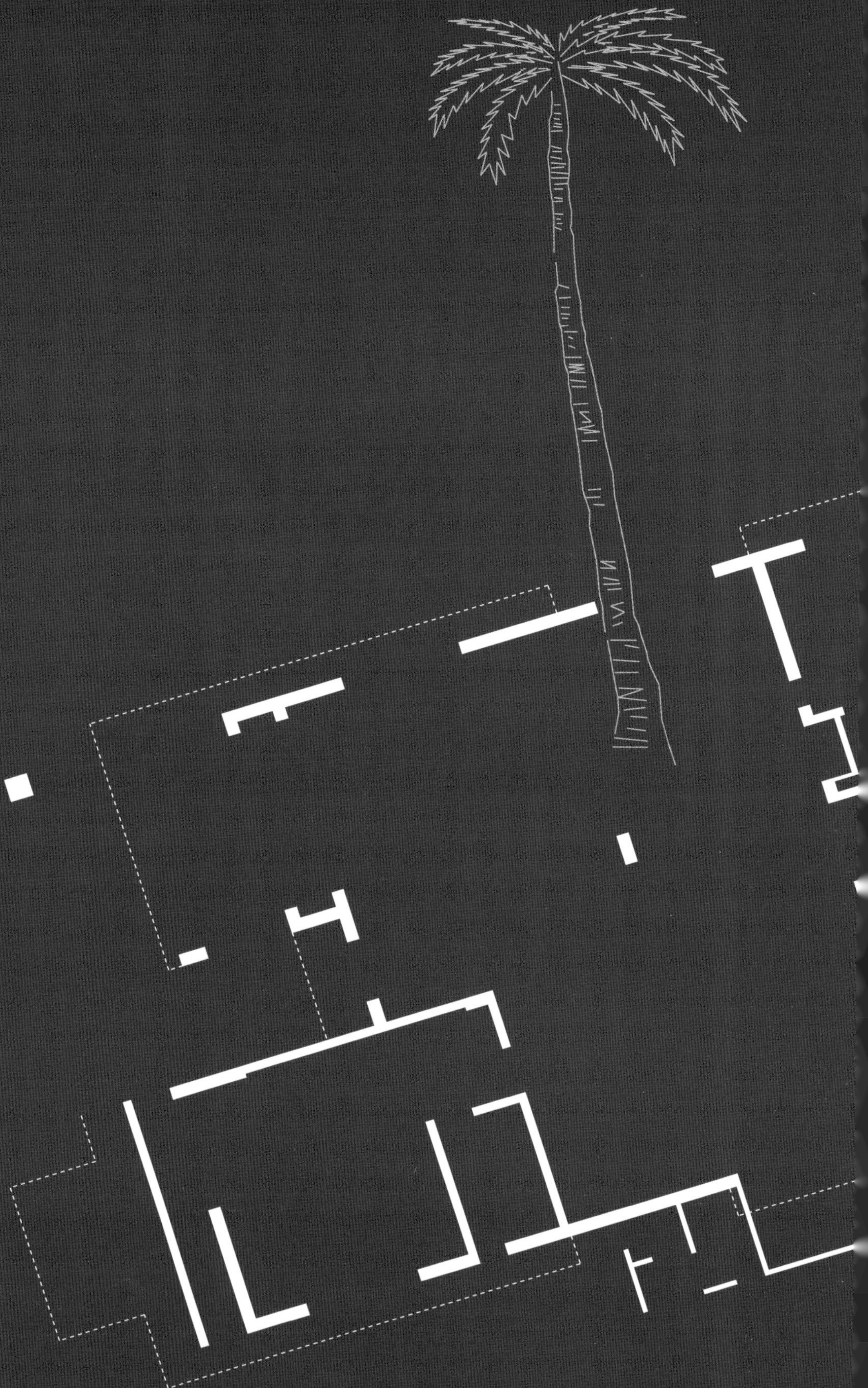

2013

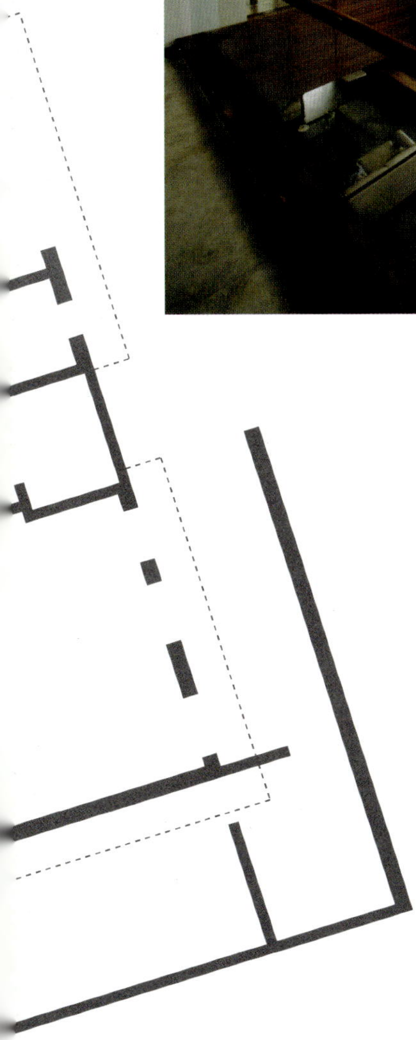

Above: The existing coconut tree included within the house.

The first impression of this house is a deceptively simple composition of lines and planes that define the shell of the building. Minimal in form and in harmony with the palm trees that intermittently dot the compact site; it creates a discreet impact. As one crosses the threshold and enters into its double height entrance lobby, a quiet transition takes place.

Play of light and a rhythmic flow of solid and void guides one towards the strong centre formed by the existing full grown coconut palm that is nestled within the house. A courtyard embraces this tree making it an integral part of the built space. A pooja room in the corner of the courtyard diagonally opposite to the tree creates a balance between the built and unbuilt.

The design grid has been evolved to fit around the existing tree, imparting a distinct spirit, a soul to the house. Discreetly tucked in bedrooms at two levels stay connected to the common areas through zen views provided by traditional louvered wada windows.

Located in an active residential neighborhood this design called for outward looking interaction spaces like balconies, verandas and large openings. Making up for the lack of space at the lower level, a roof garden is provided with raised flower beds, lush green lawns and a rustic wooden floor. These spaces are sheltered by a wooden trellis which provides a play of light and shade and is easily accessible by an elevator.

The staircase with its cantilever wooden treads is another focal point; strategically located to form a natural stage to pause on and enjoy the spaces around. A suspended cuboid emerges over the dining area adding a new dimension to the space. Interesting proportions are generated by doors and windows with enhanced lintel heights letting in ample daylight as well.

Rustic textures in muted tones of grey, beige and white, play along with handcrafted furniture in woody browns to create a harmony of colour and texture through the spaces. Line as an element in design gets interpreted at various places through the house in various details ranging from the entrance gate to the louvered wooden windows to the skylights and roof trellis.

The positivity that engulfs the space comes from its simplicity in form and the restrained use of materials. And above all, the presence of the tree within the house creates an unbroken connection from the earth to the sky above, as an intuitive response to nature.

Right: The living space flanked by the courtyard and the pooja room within.

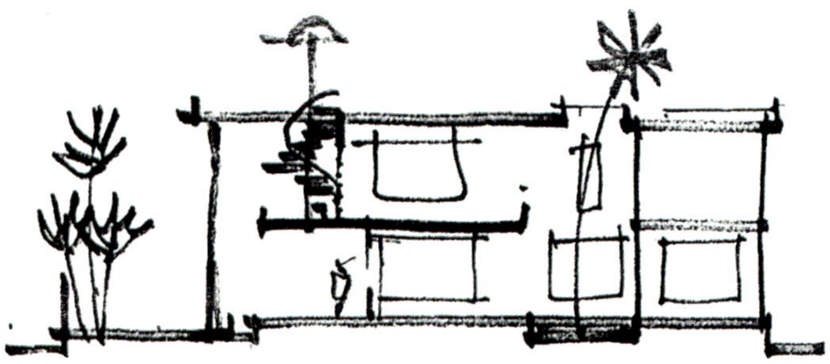

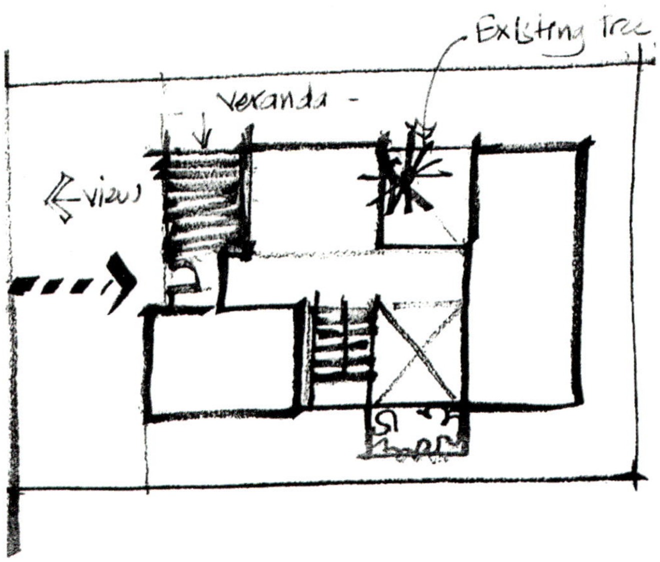

Right: Open dining space flowing into the courtyard beyond.

Left: A placid seating area on the terrace garden sheltered by a wooden trellis.

MH.15.DQ.8585

Page 270,271: A covered veranda connects the living space to a garden patch.
Page 272,273: A simple composition of lines forms the exterior with an outward looking balcony to connect to the street.
Above: Soft colours and textures highlighted by daylight.

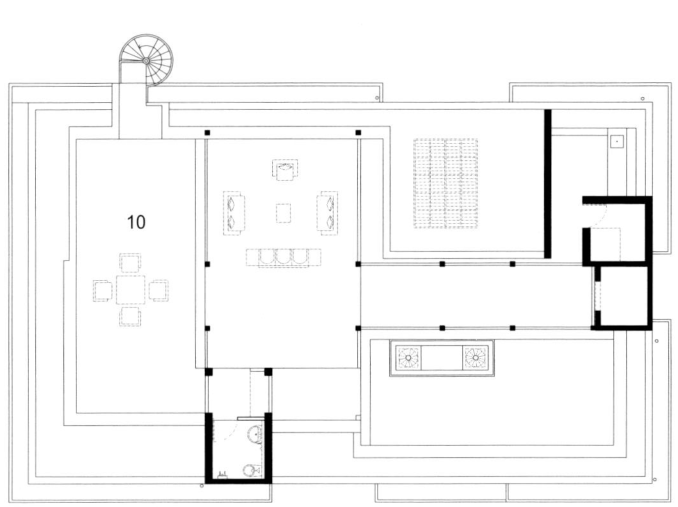

SECOND FLOOR PLAN

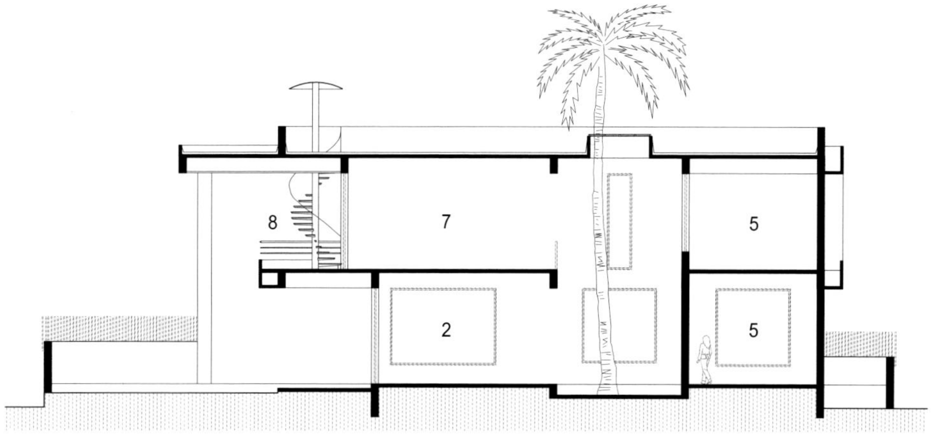

SECTION - AA'

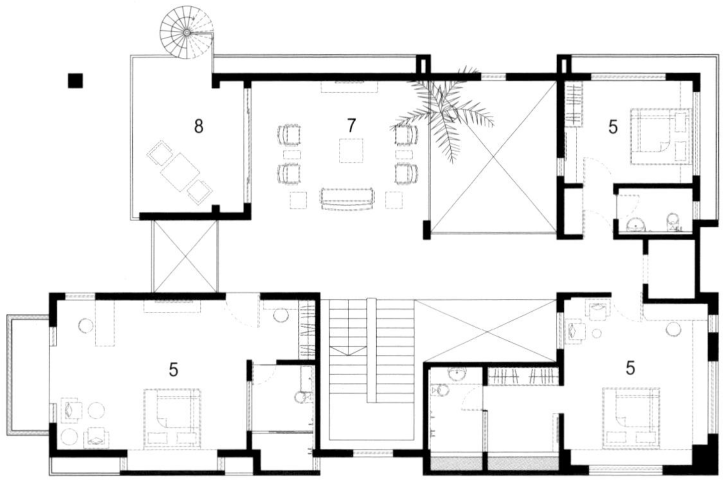

FIRST FLOOR PLAN

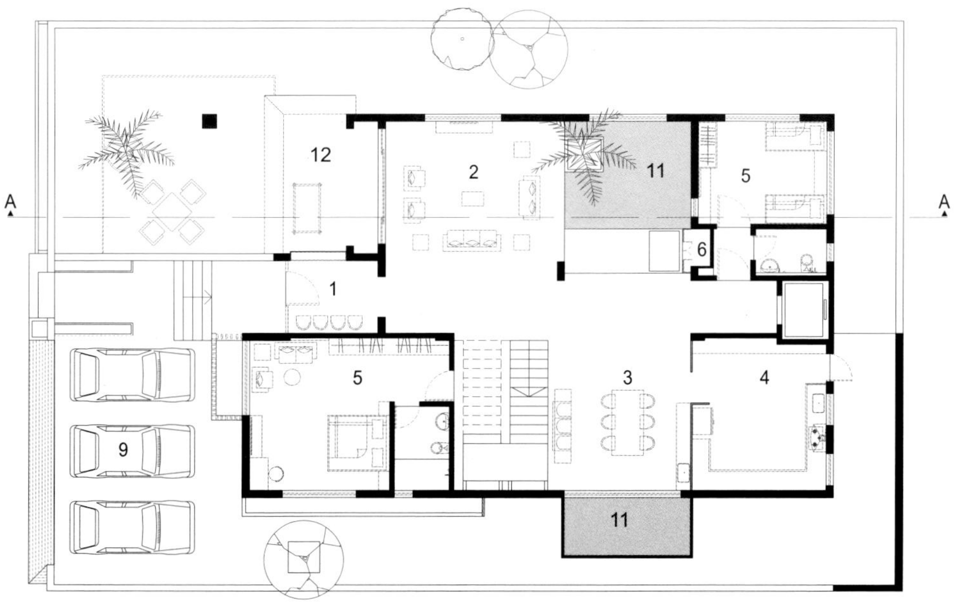

GROUND FLOOR PLAN

1.ENTRANCE LOBBY
2.LIVING ROOM
3.DINING
4.KITCHEN
5.BEDROOM
6.POOJA ROOM
7.FAMILY SEATING
8.COVERED TERRACE
9.PARKING
10.TERRACE GARDEN
11.COURT
12.COVERED VERANDAH

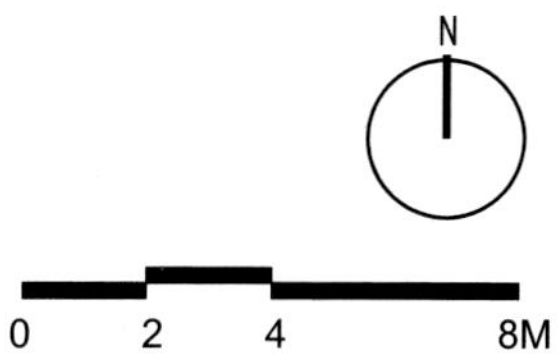

AWARDS & ACHIEVEMENTS

1990	**Dharmasthala Manjunatheshwara Award** - by Indian Institute of Architects at National Level.
1990	**Gunavantta Puraskar** - by Deshdoot daily news paper.
1993	**Outstanding Young Citizen** - by Jr. Jaycees, Nashik.
2003	**First Prize Mumbai University Sub-centre at Ratnagiri** - Competition Project.
2003	**The Building of The Year** by the Builders Association, Nashik - Anandgandha Apartments; (Category - Apartment Building).
2003	**Nashik Gaurav Puraskar**.
2006/07	**The Building of The Year** by the Builders Association, Nashik - N.D.M.V.P College of Engineering; (Category - Institutional and Green Building).
2007	A+D SPECTRUM - **Juries Special Mention Award** - Mahindra Management Development Centre, Govardhan Village, Nashik.
2008	**AESA Gold Award, Pune** - Mahindra Institute of Quality, Govardhan Village, Nashik.
2008	Third prize in **Phalke Memorial Design Competition**- organized by the Nashik Municipal Corporation at National level.
2007/09	**Best Building Of The Year** by The Builders Association (B.A.I.) of India, Nashik centre, for Mumbai Education Trust's (M.E.T.) Bhujbal Knowledge City, Nashik (Category - Institutional building).
2009	**Nomination for Aga Khan Award** - Mahindra Management Development Centre (MMDC), Nashik.
2009/11	**Best Building Of The Year** by The Builders Association (B.A.I.) of India, Nashik centre, for Y.C.M.O.U. Library and Multi-Media Centre; (Category - Government/Semi-government and Green Building).
2011/2012	Award for **Outstanding Contribution to Architectural Profession and Education**, from I.I.A. (Indian Institute of Architects Maharashtra Chapter).
2012	**Trends Excellence Awards for Architecture and Design.**
2012	**First prize - Administrative Building for Collector Office, Pune** , organized by PWD, Pune.
2012	**Artists In Concrete Awards Asia (AICA) –** Interior Designer – Sandip Foundation. (Category – Educational Building)
2012	**Artists In Concrete Awards Asia (AICA) –** Interior Designer – Y.C.M.O.U. Library. (Category – Cultural Building)
2013	**Sva Griha certificate:** Green office building designed for Green Space Realtors, received 'Sva Griha' certificate with four star rating, which is the first in Maharashtra.
2013	**Architect of the Year Award - 23rd JK AYA (2013):** Green Architecture Award for YCMOU Library and Multimedia Centre, Nashik.
2014	**Purush Sinha Award** – by Lion's Club of Nashik.
2015	**Girna Gaurav Puraskar**
2015	**Chaitra Gaurav Puraskar**
2015	**Best Building Of The Year** by The Builders Association (B.A.I.) of India, Nashik centre, for Teachers Training Institute of MVHS and VVIP Rest House, Trimbakeshwar; (Category - Institutional and Government/Semi-government).
2016	**Architect of the Year Award - 25th JK AYA (2015):** Green Architecture Award for Kusumagraj Memorial, Nashik.
2016	**Nashik Bhooshan Award** - by Rotary Club of Nashik.

CREDITS & ACKNOWLEDGEMENTS

R.C.C. Consultants:
- Jayant Bhinge
- Shailesh Dhumane
- Sanjay Ratnaparkhi
- Narayan Punjabi

Landscape Consultants:
- Apeksha Kute
- Umesh Wakaley
- Jayant Dharap
- Sanjay Patil

Services:
- Babubhai Dand
- Milind Shete
- Agnihotri-Lokhande
- Jitendra Kotwal

Contractors & Supervision Engineers:
- Rajesh Kadam
- Shrinandan Bhalerao
- Kumar Rao
- G. K. Ahire
- Rajesh Patil
- Giriraj Constructions
- Capital Constructions
- Kranti Constructions
- Parijat Constructions
- Rajhans Constructions
- Shrinath Constructions
- Harsh Constructions
- Ellora Constructions
- Unique Constructions

PUBLISHED WORKS

YEAR	PUBLICATION	PROJECT
1990 Oct	A+D Houses	Masani Residence
1998 July	Savvy	Sarada Residence
2000 Aug	Indian Architect & Builder	MMDC
2003 July	Inside Outside	Bakshi Residence, Thakkar Residence, Architect's Own Workspace
2004 March	Inside Outside	Jitubhai Thakkar's Residence
2005 Dec	Abadi Magazine, Iran	Weekend Office - Mahiravani
2004 Oct	International Symposium	Journey- In search of Integrated Spaces, Tainan University
2007 Aug	A&I Digest	Gavit Residence, Singhania Residence, Jadhav Residence, Rajubhai Thakkar Residence, Trishala Industry
2008 April	A+D	MMDC
2008 Aug	BBC GOOD HOMES	Adwait Kher Residence
2008 June	A+D	MIQ
2008 June	Indian Architecture & Builder	MIQ, Sanjeev Bafana Residence, Trishala Industry
2008 May	Inside Outside	MIQ
2008 Sept	A+D Spectrum awards	MMDC
2008 Sept	Enchante IIID magazine	MMDC
2009 Feb	Buildotech magazine	Farmhouse at Mahiravani
2009 Jan-Feb	Index furniture journal VOLUME-6	Pachpatil Farmhouse
2010 April	HOME REVIEW	Suryawanshi Residence
2010 July	Architecture Update	Raosaheb Patil Residence
2010 Nov	Inside Outside	Sandip Foundation Institute
2011 Feb	A+D	MET Institute
2011 March/ Oct	Trends	Batavia Residence / Sandip Foundation / Goliya Residence
2012 March	Lonely Planet	Beyond Resort
2012 Oct	HOME TRENDS VOL3 NO 5	Papaya Nursery
2012	Trends Award	Goliya Residence
2014 February	A+D vol 31, issue 02	Bapat Bagawe Farmhouse
	Home Review Vol 7, Issue 3	Visava Residence , Anand Residence
2015 August	Commercial Design	MET Institute, Sandip Foundation Institute, C.M.C.S, Y.C.M.O.U Library
2015 August	Home & Design Trends	MET Institute
2014 March	Home & Design Trends	Farmhouse at Mahiravani
2014 May-June	Design Matrix	Hi 5 Hotel
2014 April	Architecture	Workspace for Green Space Realtors
2014 May	HOME TRENDS	Suryavanshi Residence
2014 Dec	Commercial Design	Sandip Foundation Institute, Workspace for Green Space Realtors, YCMOU Library

Photo credits for eassys & backcover:

- Anagha Patil
- Sudhir Shingne
- Samruddha Mogal

Valuable suggestions:

- Aneev Ansari
- Ira Demedova
- Anagha Patil
- Sneha Patil

Back Cover Poem

- Minaz Ansari

Data Assimilation

- Puja Khairnar
- Ojashri Sarda
- Environ Planners' Staff

Book Layout & Graphics

- Aniket Kulkarni
- Harshjeet Chavan

A patch of earth, a fragment of sky
Brick and stone, wood and steel
Simple geometry, zen views
Pools of daylight, mounds of green...

Lessons from the past
In a language of the present
Crafted into spaces that embody
Dreams of the souls that house them...

Architecture, it is said, is not one big thing
But many small things put together
in the right measure.